A YEAR
⊰ *of* ⊱
PRAYER

John MacArthur

HARVEST HOUSE PUBLISHERS
EUGENE, OREGON

A YEAR OF PRAYER
Copyright © 2011 by John MacArthur
Published by Harvest House Publishers
Eugene, Oregon 97402
www.harvesthousepublishers.com

Library of Congress Cataloging-in-Publication Data
    MacArthur, John, 1939-
    [At the throne of grace]
    A year of prayer / John MacArthur.
        pages cm
    ISBN 978-0-7369-5865-3 (pbk.)
    ISBN 978-0-7369-5866-0 (eBook)
    1. Prayers. 2. Bible—Devotional use. I. Title.
    BV245.M14 2014
    242'.5—dc23
                                                    2013045659

CONTENTS

Prayers on the Cross and the Gospel

Prayers on Personal Holiness

Prayers on Useful Service

Appendix: Prayers on Holy Seasons

A PERSONAL WORD

*"His mercy is upon generation after generation
toward those who fear Him" (Luke 1:50).*

At an appointed moment near the beginning of the worship service, a lone figure ascends the platform stairs and approaches the pulpit. His snow-white hair speaks of a distinguished and elderly soul, yet his stride and physique reveal a younger man and the all-American athlete he was in his day. To the thousands gathered in the sanctuary, this man is their beloved pastor. Their teacher. And to many more outside the walls of this building he is a world-renowned theologian and Bible scholar. An author of esteemed repute.

To be sure, he is all of these to us as well. But John MacArthur is a man whom we love as no other. He is our dad.

We're preacher's kids. We wear the same label today that we wore as young children. And because we have been a part of a church where our dad has been the pastor since 1969, we have been surrounded all our lives by people who knew exactly who we were.

"You're Pastor MacArthur's daughter, aren't you?"

"You must be Dr. MacArthur's son; you look just like him."

As the years went by and each of us married, our spouses joined us, grafted in and belonging to the preacher. Then, one at a time, our own children became part of that family circle as well.

The preacher's extended family.

You have heard jokes about the stereotypic preacher with incorrigible kids lurking in the shadows or waiting out church services in the parking lot. Perpetual troublemakers who would prefer being anywhere but in church and *anything* but the son or daughter of the man in the pulpit.

That's not how it has been for us. Ditto the spouses and grandchildren.

Each of us has willingly drawn ourselves into the congregation that is Grace Community Church, participating in worship and volunteering for special places of service where we have been called. Our own walk with Christ has been profoundly informed by our dad's expository approach to preaching, unpacking the Word of God verse by verse.

As little ones, sitting with our mother, her open Bible and notebook reminding us what a student acted like, we read along. We listened. We took notes. As John and Patricia MacArthur's children, truth poured over us, shaping our understanding of God from the days when our feet could not reach the floor. When the time was right, we were led to kneel before a holy God and receive the gift of His salvation for ourselves.

In addition to our father's teaching gift in the pulpit, we have also been instructed and inspired by his prayers. Every Sunday at Grace Community Church, an important part of each worship service is the pastoral prayer. When the time comes for this to take place, our dad, the shepherd, steps toward the pulpit as though he's approaching the Throne of Grace. In fact, this is exactly what he is doing.

Those gathered in the sanctuary pray along silently as our dad prays with deep respect and tenderness. They quietly come alongside the man in the pulpit as he thanks God for His grace and the incomprehensible gift of Jesus. Solid theology is forged into these people as their pastor prays.

This is no casual exchange, and they know it.

For us who lived in the John and Patricia MacArthur home, the pulpit wasn't the only place that we heard our dad pray. Nearly every morning of our growing-up years, breakfast together was nearly sacramental. The morning meal our mom had painstakingly prepared was thoughtfully laid before us. No hasty bagel or splash of juice at our house. Then dad usually read a portion from Scripture and often a few paragraphs from a classic devotional. And then he would pray.

Even when we were very young, we listened attentively to our dad speak to his heavenly Father. We listened and we learned of God's grace through these humble prayers. And we began to understand who Jesus is and what He had done for us.

Our theology was shaped by the words our dad prayed.

Sitting around the kitchen table, we heard dad's words of gratitude for the privilege of being adopted into God's family. We heard expressions of his love for the Bible and the church around the world and for the people who were the congregational family at Grace Church. His transparency disclosed his own disappointments, and his faith unpacked his sheer confidence in God's providence.

In his prayers, our dad was carrying our family into the holy presence of the sovereign God of the universe.

This was no casual exchange, and we knew it.

You may have heard our dad on the radio or seen him standing in the pulpit. For our entire lifetimes, however, we have known and watched him when the microphone was unplugged all week long between Sundays. We have witnessed his tenderness with our mother, his confident discipline with us when we were disobedient or defiant adolescents. We have heard his enthusiastic cheers from the stands from T-ball to professional sports. And we have been the recipients of his affirming words and tender affection. His generosity with his calendar and resources are legendary.

By God's grace, our dad has been what he preaches.

We have seen the discipline of his pastoral study of God's Word, during which he remains focused for countless hours in preparation of opening and explaining the Scriptures to us and others.

And we have heard him pray.

A few years ago, a friend approached us and asked what we thought about our dad's prayers being transcribed and published so others could read them. We felt an immediate mix of emotions. We agreed these prayers should be put in print—and we had our children's children in mind here—but we hesitated, because we suspected that our dad would resist. We knew his thoughts regarding the sacredness and propriety of a person's personal dialogue with the Father.

So we talked it over with him. As we anticipated, dad pushed back, not enthusiastic about memorializing something so intimate. Respectfully, we asked him to pray about it and consider the loss for those who would never hear or read these prayers if they were not published. We encouraged him to allow his prayers to be available in print—not only for our own posterity but as a legacy for those of his friends around the world who would be instructed and inspired by them.

After some time, dad finally agreed...with one caveat. He asked that his children write this introductory note to the book and explain that it was our desire that he put his prayers in black and white.

As you open this book and begin to read and to experience these prayers, you will understand what we have said here about these words expressed to a sovereign God from the heart of one of His servants. These are the prayers of a warrior for Truth. For our family, these are the prayers of our dad, a gentleman who would never be presumptuous in any way. He continues his ministry to all of us from a position of humility and thanksgiving as he stands before a holy God.

And now we are pleased to be able to share these prayers with you. Because they were delivered to thousands of worshipers simultaneously by way of a microphone, they have been adapted somewhat to enhance the experience of reading them in your personal time of devotions. We hope that you'll be encouraged—and transformed—in your own time before the Throne of Grace, just as we have.

God bless you,
Matthew MacArthur
Marcy Gwinn
Mark MacArthur
Melinda Welch

PREFACE

There is great power in godly prayer. "The effectual fervent prayer of a righteous man [or woman] availeth much" (James 5:16 KJV).

You are no doubt convinced of that already since you are reading the preface to a book that seeks to lead you to the throne of grace, where God's people may receive mercy and find grace to help us in our times of need (Hebrews 4:12-16). That plural pronoun *us* is all-important because it follows the pattern established by our Lord Jesus Christ in answer to this momentous request from His disciples: "Lord, teach us to pray" (Luke 11:1). Ponder anew the comprehensive scope and majesty of what has become known as The Lord's Prayer:

- Our Father, who is in heaven, *(The Paternity of Prayer)*
- Hallowed be Your name. *(The Priority of Prayer)*
- Your kingdom come. *(The Program of Prayer)*
- Your will be done, on earth as it is in heaven. *(The Plan of Prayer)*
- Give us this day our daily bread. *(The Provision of Prayer)*
- And forgive us our debts, as we also have forgiven our debtors. *(The Pardon of Prayer)*
- And do not lead us into temptation, but deliver us from evil. *(The Protection of Prayer)*
- For Yours is the kingdom and the power and the glory forever. Amen.

Consider how strange and self-centered this would sound instead: "*My* Father, who is in heaven…Give *me* this day *my* daily bread. And forgive *me my* debts, as *I* also have forgiven *my* debtors. And do not lead *me* into temptation, but deliver *me* from evil." We who love the Lord can't help sensing that the most vital things we need to pray about go way beyond ourselves, our desires, or our own will. The Spirit within us compels us to lift up our brothers and sisters in Christ at the same time. This book is all about helping us, as God's people, to pray like that more than we actually do. Because we are fallen creatures, we wrestle constantly with a natural temptation to focus on self and immediate circumstances rather than fixing our hearts and minds on what our Lord said we *ought* to pray about. That's one of many things that make prayer such a difficult discipline for most of us.

I have been preaching from the pulpit of Grace Community Church for more than forty years now. From the very beginning, one of the most sacred and enjoyable parts of our public worship services for me has been the time when we as a congregation come together before the throne of grace. In our normal order of service each Sunday, the pastoral prayer is immediately preceded by a reading from Scripture—normally a full chapter or the equivalent. My prayers usually echo truths that are highlighted in whatever passage of Scripture we have just read together.

Many members of my flock through the years have told me that the pastoral prayer is a highlight for them each week. Over the years I have lost count of the number of people who have suggested that we should publish a collection of pastoral prayers in the form of a devotional book. Other urgent writing projects have kept me from the task until now.

In all candor, I've also been somewhat hesitant to publish a book of prayers because of the many ways prayer books can be (and often have been) abused. These prayers are not intended to be recited by rote. And I would hate to think anyone might say these prayers publicly in a merely ritualistic fashion. Remember that Jesus warned against vain repetition and showy, grandiose prayers (Matthew 6:5-8).

Remember also, however, that Jesus then immediately gave His disciples the most famous prototypical prayer of all time to teach them how to pray (verses 9-13). Clearly, there *is* a right and useful place for model prayers. They help us learn how to pray and what to pray for. They encourage and assist us in those times when "we do not know how to pray as we should" (Romans 8:26). They help us order our arguments (Job 23:4) when we want to plead our case before the throne of grace but can't seem to find the words.

Spontaneous prayer can be wonderfully passionate and expressive. Most of our praying should be the extempore outpouring of hearts that are always seeking God. But there is also a legitimate place for organizing our thoughts and planning the words we will take before God's throne—particularly when the prayer is for a time we have set aside specifically for worship, either in private or in the midst of a congregation.

Composed prayers have the advantage of being more thoughtful, more to the point, and (when used rightly) less repetitious. Here, for example, are two brief, classic prayers written by Thomas Cranmer for the Church of England's first *Book of Common Prayer*:

> Almighty and most merciful Father, we have erred and strayed from Your ways, like lost sheep. We have followed too much the devises and desires of our own hearts. We have offended against Your holy laws. We have left undone those things that we ought to have done, and we have done those things that we ought not to have done, and there is no health in us. But You, O Lord, have mercy upon us miserable offenders. Spare those, O God, who confess their faults! Restore those who are penitent according to Your promises declared to mankind in Christ Jesus our Lord. And grant, O most merciful Father, for His sake, that we may hereafter live godly, righteous, and sober lives to the glory of Your holy name. Amen.

> Almighty God, unto whom all hearts are open, all desires known, and from whom no secrets are hid: cleanse the thoughts of our hearts by the inspiration of Your Holy Spirit, that we may perfectly love You and worthily magnify Your holy name through Christ our Lord. Amen.[1]

---

1. The first prayer is a general confession. The second is a prayer of humble access. Both prayers were written by Cranmer for the 1549 edition of the prayer book. Seven years later, Cranmer was martyred for his faith when Mary Tudor, the elder daughter of King Henry VIII, made a bloody but unsuccessful attempt to destroy the English Reformation.

Notice the brevity and simple elegance of those prayers. The phrasing is wonderfully compact, and many of the expressions are borrowed directly from Scripture. Remember also that in the classic English of the King James Version, the prayer Jesus gave His disciples (Matthew 6:9-13) is only five sentences in length, comprising 66 words. In prayer, true eloquence and long-windedness are antithetical.

Despite my concern that prayer books can easily be misused in a way that fosters ritualism and religious formalism, today's evangelicals seem far more easily tempted by superficiality, self-indulgence, and prayerlessness. We need to pray more; we need to give more careful thought to the content of our prayers; and we need to spend more time preparing our hearts and our tongues for prayer. It is with that in mind that I offer this book.

These prayers are written with the hope that you will read them prayerfully. The prayers that follow have been selected from a span of several years, and the Scripture reading that preceded each prayer is included as well. To prepare your heart, carefully read the passage of Scripture first—and keep your Bible open nearby as you read each prayer. I've included a few footnotes giving cross-references to key verses that are alluded to in the words of the prayers. Follow the trail of those cross-references, and I think the exercise will deepen and enhance your prayer time.

My own preparation for prayer has often been greatly helped by resources like Spurgeon's published prayers[1] and my favorite collection of Puritan prayers, *The Valley of Vision*.[2] You may recognize some vocabulary and phrases adapted from those sources and others like them. I have benefited greatly from seeing how great men of God in earlier generations conveyed truth and passion in the simple, picturesque language they used— wholly apart from whatever nuances of expression they might have brought to their prayers through audible cues like volume, tone of voice, inflection, and emphasis. Reading some of their prayers in plain printed format is itself

---

1. C.H. Spurgeon, *The Pastor in Prayer: A Collection of the Sunday Morning Prayers of C.H. Spurgeon* (Edinburgh: Banner of Truth, 2004); *Spurgeon's Prayers* (Ross-Shire: Christian Focus, 2003).

2. Arthur G. Bennett, ed., *The Valley of Vision* (Edinburgh: Banner of Truth, 1975).

a great lesson in how to pray—and a sobering rebuke for the clumsy and slapdash way we sometimes do pray.

In my public prayers, I've always made a conscious effort not to cater to our generation's penchant for superficial, repetitious, and tacky idioms. If the prayers in this book motivate you to be more prayerful, assist you to be more expressive, or remind you to be more thoughtful in your personal prayer life, I am richly rewarded for my labors. May you be even more richly blessed by the magnificent King who invites us to His throne of grace!

Sincerely in Christ,
John MacArthur

PRAYERS ON WORSHIP AND THE ATTRIBUTES OF GOD

WEEK 1

ADORING OUR
ADVOCATE

1 John 2:1-19

My little children, I am writing these things to you so that you may not sin. And if anyone sins, we have an Advocate with the Father, Jesus Christ the righteous; and He Himself is the propitiation for our sins; and not for ours only, but also for those of the whole world.

By this we know that we have come to know Him, if we keep His commandments. The one who says, "I have come to know Him," and does not keep His commandments, is a liar, and the truth is not in him; but whoever keeps His word, in him the love of God has truly been perfected. By this we know that we are in Him: the one who says he abides in Him ought himself to walk in the same manner as He walked.

Beloved, I am not writing a new commandment to you, but an old commandment which you have had from the beginning; the old commandment is the word which you have heard. On the other hand, I am writing a new commandment to you, which is true in Him and in you, because the darkness is passing away and the true Light is already shining.

The one who says he is in the Light and yet hates his brother is in the darkness until now. The one who loves his brother abides in the Light and there is no cause for stumbling in him. But the one who hates his brother is in the darkness and walks in the darkness, and does not know where he is going because the darkness has blinded his eyes.

I am writing to you, little children, because your sins have been forgiven you for His name's sake. I am writing to you, fathers, because you know Him who has been from the beginning. I am writing to you, young men, because you have overcome the evil one. I have written to you, children, because you know the Father. I have written to you, fathers, because you know Him who has been from the beginning. I have written to you, young men, because you are strong, and the word of God abides in you, and you have overcome the evil one.

Do not love the world nor the things in the world. If anyone loves the world, the love of the Father is not in him. For all that is in the world, the lust of the flesh and the lust of the eyes and the boastful pride of life, is not from the Father, but is from the world. The world is passing away, and also its lusts; but the one who does the will of God lives forever.

Children, it is the last hour; and just as you heard that antichrist is coming, even now many antichrists have appeared; from this we know that it is the last hour. They went out from us, but they were not really of us; for if they had been of us, they would have remained with us; but they went out, so that it would be shown that they all are not of us.

OUR GRACIOUS GOD, we thank You for our heavenly Advocate,
Jesus Christ the righteous, whose death on the cross
made propitiation for all our sins—
perfectly satisfying every demand of Your holy justice.
It is He who brought us
out of guilt and into forgiveness,
out of darkness into light,
out of our rebellion and into Your love,
out of death and into life.
He delivered us from this evil world, into Your glorious kingdom.
How we praise You for the wonder of Your love in Jesus Christ!
We thank You for sending Your Son, the Incarnate One,

who was despised, rejected, beaten, mocked, and crucified—
    all in order to atone for our sin.

In Him Your love has outloved all other loves.
Your mercy extends beyond comprehension to sinners
    with complete and permanent forgiveness of our sins
    through faith in Jesus Christ.
We therefore long to love You with a love like Yours.
    We know that is not possible, so with the apostle Peter
    we plead that You would know our hearts, knowing we truly love You
        in spite of what it often looks like.[1]
Our hearts are too much like stone; we ask that
    You melt them with Your grace.
Our private lives are too often gated and locked as if we could shut You out
    and thereby do what we want.
Help us throw open the door and lose the key! May Your will rule our lives.

We worship You, Father, for Your great love and the gift of Jesus Christ,
    Your only-begotten Son, which is to say God the Son.
We praise You, Lord Jesus, for the wondrous gift of salvation
    You provided for us.
We adore You, blessed Spirit, for revealing to us the truth of the gospel
    and for making our hearts Your dwelling place.
Heavenly Father, in us may Your Son see the fruit
    of His soul's anguish and be glad.[2]
Bring us away from all that we falsely trust,
    and teach us to rest only in Him.
Never let us be calloused to the astonishing greatness of the gift of salvation.
May we pursue sanctification—ever-increasing
    holiness—with all our might!

---

1. John 21:15-17
2. Isaiah 53:10-11

Lord Jesus, Master, Redeemer, Savior, take
    possession of every part of our lives—
    Yours by right through purchase.
        Sanctify every faculty.
        Fill our hearts with hope.
        May we flee the many temptations that relentlessly hound us
            and mortify the sins that continually plague us.
        May there be no hypocrisy in us.
        Help us trust You in the hour of distress.
        Protect us when evildoers pursue us.
        And deliver us from the evil of this present world.

Dear Father of lights, with whom there is no variation or shifting shadow,
    we confess that You alone are the giver of every good and perfect gift,[1]
    and You have given us so many things,
    richly supplying us with things to enjoy.[2]
And we are reminded by the passage we have just read that
    the greatest gift of all is Your Son, Jesus Christ,
        who sacrificed His very life in order that
        we might be freed from sin's bondage.
Fill our hearts with gratitude, and may our lives
    reflect overflowing thankfulness
    so that all who see may honor You.
In the name of Jesus Christ we pray. Amen.

---

1. James 1:17
2. 1 Timothy 6:17

WEEK 2

YEARNING FOR CONSTANT WORSHIP

1 John 2:20-29

You have an anointing from the Holy One, and you all know. I have not written to you because you do not know the truth, but because you do know it, and because no lie is of the truth. Who is the liar but the one who denies that Jesus is the Christ? This is the antichrist, the one who denies the Father and the Son. Whoever denies the Son does not have the Father; the one who confesses the Son has the Father also. As for you, let that abide in you which you heard from the beginning. If what you heard from the beginning abides in you, you also will abide in the Son and in the Father. This is the promise which He Himself made to us: eternal life.

These things I have written to you concerning those who are trying to deceive you. As for you, the anointing which you received from Him abides in you, and you have no need for anyone to teach you; but as His anointing teaches you about all things, and is true and is not a lie, and just as it has taught you, you abide in Him.

Now, little children, abide in Him, so that when He appears, we may have confidence and not shrink away from Him in shame at His coming. If you know that He is righteous, you know that everyone also who practices righteousness is born of Him.

DEAR FATHER, we thank You that by Your mercy and grace,
    through the regenerating power of the Holy Spirit
    by faith in Jesus Christ, Your Son, we have come to know You.
At the moment of salvation You anointed us by Your Spirit,
    who remains forever with us to teach us to understand Your truth.[1]

You have drawn us by the power of the gospel to the light of Your Word.
You have given us grace to receive the truth—
    we who were so deeply defiled by our own guilt;
    we who were once condemned to destruction
        under the righteous demands of Your justice.
Our very souls were corrupt; we lived in rebellion against Your law;
    our minds were hostile to Your truth; and
    our very lives were an offense to Your holiness.
We were hopeless until You gave us an eternal hope.
You have saved us by Your goodness, grace, and mercy.

But You sent Your Son to be our Savior—to rescue us from sin's power
    by taking our guilt on Himself and dying to pay sin's awful price.
Mercy and truth thus met at the cross;
    righteousness and peace kissed each other.[2]
Your wrath against sin was perfectly satisfied;
Your justice was fully vindicated;
Your truth was forever established;
Your grace was brilliantly magnified;
    and all the demands of Your law were perfectly fulfilled.
In the process, You lovingly brought us
    into a place of safety, honor, glory, and everlasting salvation!
You made us Your children and heirs—
    joint heirs with Your only begotten Son.[3]
Truly "there is one God, and one mediator also

---

1. 1 John 2:27-28
2. Psalm 85:10
3. Romans 8:17

between God and men, the man Christ Jesus."[1]

As we contemplate all that Christ did for us on the cross,
     our hearts are filled with humble gratitude.
Surely He bore our grief and carried our sorrows.
He was pierced through for our transgressions,
     He was crushed for our iniquities;
     the chastening for our well-being fell upon Him;
     and by His scourging we are healed.[2]
He Himself bore our sins in His body on the cross,
     so that we might die to sin and live to righteousness.[3]
And You have graciously and tenderly drawn us to Him,
     the Shepherd and Guardian of our souls.

O Lord, what gifts these are to us!
Give us grace and pure hearts to worship in spirit and in truth,[4]
     that our praise may be acceptable to You.
May Christ Jesus be fully on display in us
     through both our words and our works,
     so that others may see and be drawn
          to the pure light of the gospel.
We ask these things in Jesus' precious name. Amen.

1. 1 Timothy 2:5
2. Isaiah 53:4-5
3. 1 Peter 2:24-25
4. John 4:23

WEEK 3

PRAISING GOD FOR
WHAT WE KNOW

1 John 5:13-20

These things I have written to you who believe in the name of the Son of God, so that you may know that you have eternal life. This is the confidence which we have before Him, that, if we ask anything according to His will, He hears us. And if we know that He hears us in whatever we ask, we know that we have the requests which we have asked from Him.

If anyone sees his brother committing a sin not leading to death, he shall ask and God will for him give life to those who commit sin not leading to death. There is a sin leading to death; I do not say that he should make request for this. All unrighteousness is sin, and there is a sin not leading to death.

We know that no one who is born of God sins; but He who was born of God keeps him, and the evil one does not touch him. We know that we are of God, and that the whole world lies in the power of the evil one. And we know that the Son of God has come, and has given us understanding so that we may know Him who is true; and we are in Him who is true, in His Son Jesus Christ. This is the true God and eternal life.

FATHER, we lift up to You the last portion of 1 John 5,
    thanking You for John's repeated uses of the word *know:*
These things are written to those who believe
    in the name of the Son of God,

so that we may *know* we have eternal life.
We *know* that You hear us in whatever we ask.
We *know* we have the requests we have asked from You
    in Jesus' name and in accordance with His will.
We *know* that no one who is born of God
    continues in the same unbroken pattern of sin as before.
We *know* that we are of God because we hear
    the voice of Your Spirit in Your Word.
And we *know* that the Son of God has come,
    and has given us understanding so that we may know
        Him who is true.

O Lord, how striking it is that we know all the *necessary* things:
    who You are, who Your Son is, what the gospel is,
    what salvation is, what sin is, what righteousness is,
    what it means to be born of God, what it means to be a child of God,
    what it means to be delivered from the power of the evil one,
    what it means to have eternal life.
These things we know because
    You have given us revelation and illuminated our understanding
        so that we might know with full assurance.

The best of it all is knowing You—
    the God of all comfort,
    Father of mercies,
    our ever-present God,
    eternal Savior,
    Creator of heaven and earth,
    Lord of righteousness,
    judge of all things,
    and justifier of all who believe in Jesus—
        how unsearchable are Your judgments
        and unfathomable Your ways![1]

---

1. Romans 11:33

You are unspeakably great, and greatly to be praised.[1]
The eyes of all look to You, and You give them their food in due time.
You open Your hand and satisfy the desire of every living thing.[2]
May we seek satisfaction in You alone.

We bless You for the good news of salvation—
    all its doctrines, insights, promises, and pleadings.
By its truth we understand that we were hopelessly lost,
    but You sought and found us.
We were poor and empty, but You have filled our cups to overflowing.
We were in darkness, but You brought us into the light.
We were in bondage to sin, but You bought us
    and made us slaves to righteousness.
You became for us a place of refuge—
    our fortress, our Rock, and our redeemer.

Make us to be bold reflections of the grace and holiness
    embodied in Your Son, our Savior, the Lord Jesus Christ.
Use both our lives and our lips to tell the world of His glory.

We know that all things are in Your hands. You will not permit us
    to be tempted beyond what we are able,[3] and You can use even
    the worst calamities of this life for our good and Your eternal glory.[4]
Yet we pray as Christ Himself instructed us to pray: Deliver us from evil.
See us safely and speedily through all the trials
    that are so common in this life,
    and deliver us from temptation.

Forgive us, Lord, for this week's sins. Wash us; make us clean
    even as we worship You now.
In Your Son's name we pray,
    thanking You again for what we know. Amen.

---

1. Psalm 145:3
2. Psalm 145:15-16
3. 1 Corinthians 10:13
4. Genesis 50:19-20; Romans 8:28; Ephesians 1:11-12

PURSUING CHRIST'S PERFECT RIGHTEOUSNESS

ROMANS 2:1-8

Y ou have no excuse, everyone of you who passes judgment, for in that
which you judge another, you condemn yourself; for you who judge
practice the same things. And we know that the judgment of God rightly
falls upon those who practice such things. But do you suppose this, O man,
when you pass judgment on those who practice such things and do the same
yourself, that you will escape the judgment of God? Or do you think lightly
of the riches of His kindness and tolerance and patience, not knowing that
the kindness of God leads you to repentance? But because of your stubbornness and unrepentant heart you are storing up wrath for yourself in the day
of wrath and revelation of the righteous judgment of God, who will render
to each person according to his deeds: to those who by perseverance in doing
good seek for glory and honor and immortality, eternal life; but to those who
are selfishly ambitious and do not obey the truth, but obey unrighteousness,
wrath and indignation.

LORD OF GLORY, we know that You are a righteous God
who holds every person justly responsible for his or her own sins.
This is consistent with Your holy nature.
We cannot condemn the sins of others

without condemning our own selves, for we are not free from sin.
We deserve Your judgment, yet You withhold that judgment
    because You are rich in kindness, longsuffering, tolerance,
    and patience for the purpose of leading us to repentance.
You mercifully warn us that those who remain
    unrepentant are storing up wrath
    for that final day when the fullness of Your wrath will be revealed.

We know that in the end everyone will be brought
    before Your judgment throne.
The passage we have just read says those who do evil will perish,
    and those who do good will enter into eternal life.
We confess that we have done evil,
    and we stand in need of Your grace and forgiveness.

Yet Your Word also teaches from cover to cover that salvation
    is not a reward for good works; eternal life is granted to sinners like us
        by grace alone through faith alone.
We furthermore know and freely confess
    that the good works done by believers
        are *fruits* of Your saving work, not the cause of it.
So our only claim to heaven is grounded in the promise that
    Christ is our righteousness;[1]
    His own perfection covers believers like a spotless garment.

We also confess that it is not within our capability
    to do anything truly good or contribute any merit toward our salvation.
Left completely to ourselves, we would do nothing but evil.
Even the very best of our works are flawed by fleshly imperfections
    and tainted with mixed motives.

Thus we understand and confess that those whom this text speaks of
    as "doing good" receive eternal life because of *Christ's* work,
    not as a reward for their own works.

---

1. Jeremiah 23:5-6; 33:16; Romans 4:6; 1 Corinthians 1:30

Whatever is truly good in any of our deeds is the fruit of
>Your grace and empowerment.[1]

Our hope therefore lies not in any merit or good works of our own.
We trust Christ alone for salvation,
>and we humbly and fervently pray that
>>our lives might reflect His character,
>>show forth the glory of His righteousness,
>>and be living examples of His goodness.
Clothe us not only in His righteousness, but also in
>His wisdom, His virtue, His holiness, and His humility.
Conform us perfectly to His image, according to Your eternal purpose.

We do not deserve such favor. On the contrary, our only plea
>is that of the publican who prayed,
>>"God, be merciful to me, the sinner!"[2]
And when we come to that final judgment, may we be found in Christ—
>and therefore in the company of the One who,
>>by perseverance in doing good,
>>sought for glory and honor and immortality on our behalf.
In the words of the apostle Paul, may we be found in Christ,
>not having a righteousness of our own derived from the law,
>but that which is through faith in Christ,
>>the righteousness which comes from God
>>on the basis of faith.

We ask these things in the name of our Lord Jesus Christ,
>who lived and died and rose again
>in order that we might have life. Amen.

---

1. Titus 3:5; Ephesians 2:8-10
2. Luke 18:13

LOVING THE LORD OF THE LAW

ROMANS 7:1-12

D*o you not know, brethren (for I am speaking to those who know the law), that the law has jurisdiction over a person as long as he lives? For the married woman is bound by law to her husband while he is living; but if her husband dies, she is released from the law concerning the husband. So then, if while her husband is living she is joined to another man, she shall be called an adulteress; but if her husband dies, she is free from the law, so that she is not an adulteress though she is joined to another man.*

Therefore, my brethren, you also were made to die to the Law through the body of Christ, so that you might be joined to another, to Him who was raised from the dead, in order that we might bear fruit for God. For while we were in the flesh, the sinful passions, which were aroused by the Law, were at work in the members of our body to bear fruit for death. But now we have been released from the Law, having died to that by which we were bound, so that we serve in newness of the Spirit and not in oldness of the letter.

What shall we say then? Is the Law sin? May it never be! On the contrary, I would not have come to know sin except through the Law; for I would not have known about coveting if the Law had not said, "You shall not covet." But sin, taking opportunity through the commandment, produced in me coveting of every kind; for apart from the Law sin is dead. I was once alive apart from the Law; but when the commandment came, sin became alive and I died; and this commandment, which was to result in life, proved to result in death for me; for sin, taking an opportunity through the

*commandment, deceived me and through it killed me. So then, the Law is
holy, and the commandment is holy and righteous and good.*

OUR FATHER, we have been blessed by the
    enlightening ministry of Your Spirit,
    who has opened our understanding to grasp the glories of the gospel.
By Him we understand that Your moral law
    is "holy and righteous and good,"
    a manifestation of Your holy nature.
        As such it is perfect and unchanging.
    We love the law because it is an expression of Your very Self.

But we confess that we have sinned and therefore the law cannot save us.
By the works of the law no flesh will be justified in Your sight;
    because through the law comes the knowledge of sin.[1]
We cannot merit redemption from sin or ransom ourselves
    from the bondage of evil by our own works,
    because we have already fallen far short of the perfection
        Your law requires—and thus under the law
        we stand condemned already.[2]

We thank You that You have opened another way:
    "the righteousness of God through faith in Jesus Christ,"
    who perfectly obeyed the law on our behalf.[3]
Although the law was established as a true
    reflection of Your absolute holiness,
    it is not given to us as a means of salvation,
    but rather as a means of revealing our sin

---

1. Romans 3:20
2. John 3:18
3. Romans 3:22

so we can run to Christ for mercy and through faith
obtain the salvation He purchased on the cross for us.

We are overwhelmed, we are grateful, and we worship You now in prayer
because of Your gift of full and free redemption
through faith in Jesus Christ.
You have covered us with Your own righteousness,
Christ having paid in full the penalty for our sins.
Since all the condemnation we deserved
was poured out on Him at the cross,
none is left for us!
You exacted the just penalty for sin on Your own Son,
and You, renowned as Judge of all the earth,
are the justifier of all who believe in Him.[1]

We glory in this Gospel, O Lord of the law, and we love You for it!
We ask, as a token of our love, that You would cause us
to live in the light of it.
We know that we are often unfaithful; we fail and our flesh is weak.
We sin and so again we ask for daily forgiveness and cleansing.
Make us in practice what we are before You in position.
Grant to us increasing practical righteousness and holiness.
By Your Word and Spirit mold us into the very image of Christ,
in whose name we pray. Amen.

1. Romans 3:26

REFLECTING ON
THE POWER OF ONE

ROMANS 5:12-21

J ust as through one man sin entered into the world, and death through sin, so death spread to all men, because all sinned—for until the Law sin was in the world, but sin is not imputed when there is no law. Nevertheless death reigned from Adam until Moses, even over those who had not sinned in the likeness of the offense of Adam, who is a type of Him who was to come.

But the free gift is not like the transgression. For if by the transgression of the one the many died, much more did the grace of God and the gift by the grace of the one Man, Jesus Christ, abound to the many. The gift is not like that which came through the one who sinned; for on the one hand the judgment arose from one transgression resulting in condemnation, but on the other hand the free gift arose from many transgressions resulting in justification. For if by the transgression of the one, death reigned through the one, much more those who receive the abundance of grace and of the gift of righteousness will reign in life through the One, Jesus Christ.

So then as through one transgression there resulted condemnation to all men, even so through one act of righteousness there resulted justification of life to all men. For as through the one man's disobedience the many were made sinners, even so through the obedience of the One the many will be made righteous. The Law came in so that the transgression would increase; but where sin increased, grace abounded all the more, so that, as sin reigned in death, even so grace would reign through righteousness to eternal life through Jesus Christ our Lord.

Dear heavenly Father, You are
   faithful and true, holy and righteous,
   yet full of grace and compassion—the Most High God.
We are wretched, sinful, fallen creatures, utterly unworthy of Your favor.
Yet You sent Your own beloved Son to do for us what Adam failed to do:
   to fulfill the law perfectly;
   to die in our place;
   to redeem us from our hopeless state—
      to lift us up from Adam's fall.
In Adam we were spiritually dead and headed for eternal condemnation;
   in Christ we are made alive eternally.[1]

As by Adam, sin entered the world, and death by sin, even so by Christ
   we receive Your grace, forgiveness, righteousness, and eternal life.
Christ did everything Adam ought to have done, and more—
   elevating us to a state of justification and divine favor
      no mere creature could ever hope to merit.
Our guilt was imputed to Him, and He atoned for it;
   likewise, His perfect righteousness is imputed to us,
   and we are rewarded for it.
We stand before You now as Your own adopted children,
   joint heirs with Christ.[2]
There are no words adequate to express our wonder and thankfulness
   for so great salvation.

We come to You in the name of Christ,
   the perfect mediator between God and men—
   fully human, yet eternally God.

1. 1 Corinthians 15:22
2. Romans 8:17

Your Word teaches us that although He always existed in the form of God,
   He did not regard equality with God a thing to be grasped.
For our sake He made Himself nothing, becoming truly and fully human,[1]
   so He could reverse the failure of Adam and be the head
      of a new, redeemed race.
Since we are made of flesh and blood,
   Christ Himself also partook of the same,
   that through death He might render powerless
   him who had the power of death, that is, the devil,
      and thus become a merciful and faithful high priest in things
         pertaining to God, to make propitiation for the sins of His people.[2]

Now He is our true Head and High Priest—
   One who can sympathize with our weakness.[3]
For since He Himself was tempted in that which He has suffered,
   He is able to come to the aid of those who are tempted.[4]

We thank You, dear Father, that as sin formerly reigned over us,
   now grace reigns through Jesus Christ.
   Divine grace has transformed us.
We have been taken out of the curse brought
   upon us through the sin of Adam,
   and we have been placed under Your blessing through Christ.
That is why we worship You and seek to live lives that honor You.
Be pleased, Lord, as we offer You this prayer of thanksgiving
   for the gifts of forgiveness, justification, righteousness, salvation,
   and eternal life, which come in Jesus Christ. Amen.

---

1. Philippians 2:6-7
2. Hebrews 2:14-17
3. Hebrews 4:15
4. Hebrews 2:18

REFLECTING ON GOD'S FAITHFULNESS

ROMANS 11:25-36

I do not want you, brethren, to be uninformed of this mystery—so that you will not be wise in your own estimation—that a partial hardening has happened to Israel until the fullness of the Gentiles has come in; and so all Israel will be saved; just as it is written, "The Deliverer will come from Zion, He will remove ungodliness from Jacob. This is My covenant with them, when I take away their sins."

From the standpoint of the gospel they are enemies for your sake, but from the standpoint of God's choice they are beloved for the sake of the fathers; for the gifts and the calling of God are irrevocable. For just as you once were disobedient to God, but now have been shown mercy because of their disobedience, so these also now have been disobedient, that because of the mercy shown to you they also may now be shown mercy. For God has shut up all in disobedience so that He may show mercy to all.

Oh, the depth of the riches both of the wisdom and knowledge of God! How unsearchable are His judgments and unfathomable His ways! For who has known the mind of the Lord, or who became His counselor? Or who has first given to Him that it might be paid back to him again? For from Him and through Him and to Him are all things. To Him be the glory forever. Amen.

OUR FATHER, we thank You that You are a covenant-keeping God.
Your Word gives us the wonderful example of ethnic Israel,
    whom You will one day save according to Your promise.
We thank You that even now there is only a partial spiritual hardening,
    for there are many true Israelites[1] who have come to faith
        in Jesus as Messiah.
And when "the fullness of the Gentiles" is complete—
    before the final in-gathering of people into the church
    from every nation, tongue, and tribe—
        then You will fulfill Your promise to Israel.
This is Your covenant: When they see their nail-pierced
    Messiah return in His glory,
    a fountain will be opened for the house of David and for
        the inhabitants of Jerusalem, to wash away sin and impurity.[2]
Your Word and Your covenants are always true and trustworthy,
    for the gifts and the calling of God are irrevocable.[3]

All nations of the earth are beneficiaries of Your grace even in the wake
    of Israel's disobedience, for when that nation rejected the Lord Jesus
        as their promised Messiah, You turned to the Gentiles.[4]
And when You have accomplished Your sovereign work among the nations,
    You will turn again to Israel and show mercy to them
        just as You have to the Gentiles.
That prompts us to marvel with the apostle Paul,
    O, the depth of the riches both of Your wisdom and knowledge!
    For from You and through You and to You are all things
        and the glory forever!

Thank You for the grace of salvation to both Jew and Gentile.
How grateful we are from the depths of our being to You,

---

1. John 1:47
2. Zechariah 12:8–13:1
3. Romans 11:29
4. Cf. Acts 13:46; Isaiah 55:3-7; Hosea 1:10

Lord Jesus, for bearing our sin in Your own body on the cross.[1]
Your self-sacrifice is the guarantee of our redemption,
>   the reason for our hope,
>   the ground of our assurance, and
>   the song of our faith.
Your death purchased our salvation,
>   Your resurrection guarantees our justification, and
>   Your intercession at the throne of grace secures our perseverance.

Teach us, Lord, to walk obediently by faith.
Empower us through Your Spirit to live in Your strength.
May we gladly bear the yoke that is easy and the burden that is light.[2]
And may we wear that yoke faithfully until we see You face-to-face.
In the meantime, enable us to be truly useful in the advancement
>   of Your kingdom.
What a privilege this is for us—
>   that You overcome our fallenness, wretchedness, sinfulness,
>   weakness, and ignorance to transform us into
>   instruments of Your grace in this world!

Be honored, Lord, as we offer You our worship in reflecting on
>   Your faithfulness to Your people.
We pray for the glory of the Lord Jesus Christ,
>   and in His mighty name. Amen.

---

1. 1 Peter 2:24
2. Matthew 11:28-30

WEEK 8

PRAISING GOD ALONE

Psalm 146

Praise the LORD!
  Praise the LORD, O my soul!
I will praise the LORD while I live;
I will sing praises to my God while I have my being.
Do not trust in princes,
In mortal man, in whom there is no salvation.
His spirit departs, he returns to the earth;
In that very day his thoughts perish.

How blessed is he whose help is the God of Jacob,
Whose hope is in the LORD his God,
Who made the heaven and earth,
The sea and all that is in them;
Who keeps faith forever;
Who executes justice for the oppressed;
Who gives food to the hungry.
The LORD sets the prisoners free.

The LORD opens the eyes of the blind;
The LORD raises up those who are bowed down;
The LORD loves the righteous;
The LORD protects the strangers;
He supports the fatherless and the widow,
But He thwarts the way of the wicked.

The LORD will reign forever,
Your God, O Zion, to all generations.
Praise the LORD!

ETERNAL GOD AND HEAVENLY FATHER,

we echo the psalmist: Praise the Lord!
We have not put our trust in human leaders, in mortal beings;
in them there is no salvation.
But we have put our trust in You, the Lord our God,
Creator of heaven and earth.
You are forever faithful. One day You will bring perfect justice
throughout the earth.

In the meantime, You provide for all the needs of Your people.
We thank You that You have filled the hungry, liberated captives,
given sight to the blind, raised up those who are bowed down,
and comforted those who are oppressed.
Indeed, how blessed is he whose help is the God of Jacob,
whose hope is in the Lord his God!
We thank You that You love perfectly and everlastingly
those who are covered with Your righteousness.
We worship You, Lord, as the Maker and Sustainer of all things.
We give thanks to You, O God; we glorify You for Your wondrous deeds![1]

As blessed as we are to be under the cover of Your grace, however,
we must confess that we have sinned. We have broken Your law,
which is written in our hearts as well as in the Scriptures.
We have disregarded the voice of conscience and spurned
the clear direction of Your Spirit. Worse yet, we have at times
refused the clear commands of Your holy Word.

---

1. Psalm 75:1

Yet You daily show us grace and longsuffering,
     and in Christ we are forgiven.
Purge our lives of sin,
     cleanse our souls from guilt,
     deliver us from earthly affections,
     guide our feet away from the path of evil,
     and make us walk in the way of righteousness,
          for the sake of Your holy Name.
May we pursue the beauty of Your holiness
     and the security of the hope You have set before us.
May we never lose our firm assurance in a salvation that is forever.

Thank You for equipping us with suitable spiritual armor to protect us
     against the wiles of the evil one.[1]
Thank You for such a great High Priest,
     who intercedes for us always.[2]
Thank You for Your Word,
     which guides and teaches us.
Graciously empower us to bind it upon our hearts,
     and thus to set our minds on You.
We long to understand Your truths and to observe how You operate
     so we can see blessing in every trial and joy in every sorrow.

Fill our hearts with gratitude and praise,
     and may we see Your design in everything!
Cause us, Lord, to proclaim Your Gospel to all who will hear—
     and may we gain a better hearing because both our doctrine
     and our practice manifest the glory of Christ in His saving work.
In every condition of life,
          whether we struggle or prosper,
          suffer or rejoice,

1. Ephesians 6:10-20
2. Romans 8:34; Hebrews 7:25

may we know that in Your hands all these
    things are being worked together
for our good and Your eternal glory.[1]
We are privileged to be called Your children, and we pour out our hearts
    in prayer to You, loving Father.
In the name of Your Son we pray. Amen.

---

1. Romans 8:28-30

ADORING GOD FOR HIS CREATION AND HIS WORD

PSALM 19:1-14

The heavens are telling of the glory of God;
And their expanse is declaring the work of His hands.
Day to day pours forth speech,
And night to night reveals knowledge.
There is no speech, nor are there words;
Their voice is not heard.
Their line has gone out through all the earth,
And their utterances to the end of the world.
In them He has placed a tent for the sun,
Which is as a bridegroom coming out of his chamber;
It rejoices as a strong man to run his course.
Its rising is from one end of the heavens,
And its circuit to the other end of them;
And there is nothing hidden from its heat.

The law of the LORD is perfect, restoring the soul;
The testimony of the LORD is sure, making wise the simple.
The precepts of the LORD are right, rejoicing the heart;
The commandment of the LORD is pure, enlightening the eyes.
The fear of the LORD is clean, enduring forever;
The judgments of the LORD are true; they are righteous altogether.

They are more desirable than gold, yes, than much fine gold;
Sweeter also than honey and the drippings of the honeycomb.

Moreover, by them Your servant is warned;
In keeping them there is great reward.
Who can discern his errors? Acquit me of hidden faults.
Also keep back Your servant from presumptuous sins;
Let them not rule over me;
Then I will be blameless,
And I shall be acquitted of great transgression.
Let the words of my mouth and the meditation of my heart
Be acceptable in Your sight,
O LORD, my rock and my Redeemer.

O FATHER, the heavens speak clearly of Your incomprehensible glory,
and their expanse declares repeatedly the work of Your hands:
"Day to day pours forth speech, and night to night reveals knowledge"
of You, our awesome Creator—
and this is speech that everyone can understand.
The sun moves under Your direction in a vast circuit.
Your glory is on display throughout our solar system and beyond,
from one end of the heavens to the other.
We are in awe of Your incomprehensible power.

And yet even more wonderful to us than Your glorious creation
is the revelation of Yourself in Scripture:
Your law, testimony, precepts, commandments, and judgments,
all of which are perfect, sure, right, pure, clean, and true.
Your Word converts the soul, makes us wise,
brings us joy, enlightens us,
and produces righteousness in us.

We therefore desire Your Word more than
    gold, finding it sweeter than honey.

Precious heavenly Father, all our delight is in You.
The deepest longing of our hearts is to see and to celebrate Your glory.
We will not be truly satisfied
    until we behold Your face in righteousness.[1]
That is why we now pour out our love and worship to You in prayer.
    We trust in Your promises,
    rejoice in Your faithfulness,
    glory in Your goodness,
    hope in Your Word,
    believe in Your Son,
    and rest in Your grace.

Thank You for enabling us to rest in full assurance.
We know that past, present, and future are all in Your care.
We joyfully confess that Your plan is best,
    Your commandments are just,
    Your wisdom is flawless,
    Your power is supreme,
    and all Your ways are perfect.
You are full of lovingkindness, merciful, holy, upright, and gracious—
    the fountain of all that is truly good.
We yield to You as our King and our Redeemer,
    asking that Your will be done in us.

Give us hearts that trust without sighing or complaining
    about what Your providence brings into our lives.
Shower us with mercy and grace, as You always do,
    and may we live in constant gratitude.
Whenever we sin and act in a rebellious way,
    help us to recognize our folly quickly and repent.

---

1. Psalm 17:15

Then take away our mournful sorrow and
    emblazon our hearts with gladness.
    Fill our hearts with holy songs of praise.
    Restore us that we might be beacons of Your grace.
We come to worship You, Father, relying on Your forgiveness and power
    that we might enter Your presence
    and be welcomed as true worshipers.[1]
We come in the name of our Savior. Amen.

---

1. John 4:23-24

PRAISING FATHER, SON, AND HOLY SPIRIT

EPHESIANS 5:25-32

Husbands, love your wives, just as Christ also loved the church and gave Himself up for her, so that He might sanctify her, having cleansed her by the washing of water with the word, that He might present to Himself the church in all her glory, having no spot or wrinkle or any such thing; but that she would be holy and blameless. So husbands ought also to love their own wives as their own bodies. He who loves his own wife loves himself; for no one ever hated his own flesh, but nourishes and cherishes it, just as Christ also does the church, because we are members of His body. For this reason a man shall leave his father and mother and shall be joined to his wife, and the two shall become one flesh. This mystery is great; but I am speaking with reference to Christ and the church.

OUR GREAT HEAVENLY FATHER,
    blessed Son, and eternal Spirit,
we come to worship You—God in three Persons,
      one in essence,
      perfect in every way,
      the only true God.
Our hearts are filled with gratitude for the redemption our heavenly Father

has furnished for us in Christ the Son
and applied to us by the Holy Spirit.
Undeserving though we are, You have welcomed us
into Your everlasting Kingdom,
so that we might be partakers of Your unspeakable glory.

Again, Father, we thank You that in the fullness of Your grace,
You loved us and sent Your only begotten Son to redeem us.

Lord Jesus, though existing eternally in the form of God,
You did not count that as something to be clung to.
You humbled Yourself, took on the form of a servant,
and were made in the likeness of men.
As a man, You became a servant, being obedient to the Father's will—
even unto death on the cross. [1]
That one sacrifice atoned for our sins forever
and provided us with a covering such as we needed—
the spotless garment of Your perfect righteousness.

Holy Spirit, You too have loved us everlastingly,
and now You make Your permanent abode in our hearts,
letting Your life and power flow through us,
producing abundant fruit and conforming
us to the image of Christ.

O God—one God yet three Persons—we praise You and thank You
for mercy so undeserved, and for grace beyond measure.
Your lovingkindness is inexhaustible;
Your mercies endure forever;
Your faithfulness extends to all generations;
Your glory is seen in all Your works;
and Your steadfast love is our song.

---

1. Philippians 2:7-8

We come to You, the triune God,
      enthroned in our lives,
      presiding over the universe,
    and we humbly ask for You to strengthen us where we are weak,
    beginning with our acts of worship.
You who spoke the universe into existence with but a word
    are the One who has shone in our hearts
      to give the Light of the knowledge of the glory of God
      in the face of Christ.[1]
How we thank You again for commanding salvation on our behalf!

Lord, we come before You in prayer to bring You our praise.
Set our lives in order before You,
    and renew our commitment to love and obedience,
      usefulness and faithfulness.
Be honored through our lives, we pray,
    in the name of Christ. Amen.

---

1. 2 Corinthians 4:6

SINGING PRAISE TO GOD OUTWARDLY AND INWARDLY

Psalm 148–150

*P*raise the Lord!
　　Praise the Lord from the heavens;
Praise Him in the heights!
Praise Him, all His angels;
Praise Him, all His hosts!
Praise Him, sun and moon;
Praise Him, all stars of light!
Praise Him, highest heavens,
And the waters that are above the heavens!
Let them praise the name of the Lord,
For He commanded and they were created.
He has also established them forever and ever;
He has made a decree which will not pass away.

Praise the Lord from the earth,
Sea monsters and all deeps;
Fire and hail, snow and clouds;
Stormy wind, fulfilling His word;
Mountains and all hills;
Fruit trees and all cedars;
Beasts and all cattle;

Creeping things and winged fowl;
Kings of the earth and all peoples;
Princes and all judges of the earth;
Both young men and virgins;
Old men and children.

Let them praise the name of the LORD,
For His name alone is exalted;
His glory is above earth and heaven.
And He has lifted up a horn for His people,
Praise for all His godly ones;
Even for the sons of Israel, a people near to Him.
Praise the LORD!

Praise the LORD!
Sing to the LORD a new song,
And His praise in the congregation of the godly ones.
Let Israel be glad in his Maker;
Let the sons of Zion rejoice in their King.
Let them praise His name with dancing;
Let them sing praises to Him with timbrel and lyre.
For the LORD takes pleasure in His people;
He will beautify the afflicted ones with salvation.

Let the godly ones exult in glory;
Let them sing for joy on their beds.
Let the high praises of God be in their mouth,
And a two-edged sword in their hand,
To execute vengeance on the nations
And punishment on the peoples,
To bind their kings with chains
And their nobles with fetters of iron,
To execute on them the judgment written;
This is an honor for all His godly ones.
Praise the LORD!

Praise the Lord!
Praise God in His sanctuary;
Praise Him in His mighty expanse.
Praise Him for His mighty deeds;
Praise Him according to His excellent greatness.

Praise Him with trumpet sound;
Praise Him with harp and lyre.
Praise Him with timbrel and dancing;
Praise Him with stringed instruments and pipe.
Praise Him with loud cymbals;
Praise Him with resounding cymbals.
Let everything that has breath praise the Lord.
Praise the Lord!

O LORD, in focusing our prayers heavenward
    and considering the majestic theme of worship,
    we naturally turn to the book of Psalms.
    The final five psalms in our psalter all begin,
        "Praise the Lord!"
    Indeed, Lord, You are worthy of this great crescendo,
    this ringing, jubilant call to praise
        that echoes throughout the ages.

We add our voices to the eternal choir in praise of Your holy name,
    for You alone are exalted forever.
Your glory is above earth and heaven,
    far above everything You have made.
We Your people therefore join together in prayer
    and sing to You "a new song," which is the song of redemption.[1]

---

1. Revelation 5:9-14

Father, these psalms enjoin lively praise,
    employing all that we are and have—
    along with stringed, wind, and percussion instruments;
    in the dance; and with every ounce of our breath.
In fact, the concluding verse of the final psalm is,
    "Let everything that has breath praise the LORD.
    Praise the LORD!"[1]

We realize that when these psalms were first penned and sung,
        the redemption they celebrate
        was understood only through Your promise.
    It was explained through types and shadows—
        with so much of what was to come
            still veiled in darkness.

But now Christ has brought life and immortality
    to light through the gospel.[2]
Now through the atoning work of Christ,
    we understand the mystery of salvation—
        that on the cross, He rendered a blood sacrifice,
        to be received by faith—
            not earned with any merit of our own.[3]

For we have no merit.
We are fallen, sinful, needy, helpless sinners—
    with no ability to free ourselves from the bondage of our sin
    and therefore incapable of earning Your favor
        through any works of our own.
But Christ has supplied the righteousness we need,
    and Your Word promises
        that all who call on His name will be saved.[4]

1. Psalm 150:6
2. 2 Timothy 1:10
3. Romans 3:25
4. Romans 10:13

We claim that promise by faith,
    filled with profound gratefulness
        that all Your promises in Christ are yea and amen.[1]

On this side of the cross, therefore, our praise
    is enriched, enhanced, and enlarged,
    since it encompasses the great glory
        of the incarnate Son of God
            in His mighty work at Calvary.
We are greatly blessed to have this full picture,
    and offer You our praise
    with profound yet humble gratitude.
May a song ring from our hearts at all times
    because of the greatness of the salvation
        You have given to us in Your Son,
        in whose name we pray. Amen.

---

1. 2 Corinthians 1:20

PRAYERS ON
JOY AND LONGING

WEEK 12

KNOWING TRUE JOY

PSALM 95:1-11

O come, let us sing for joy to the LORD,
  Let us shout joyfully to the rock of our salvation.
Let us come before His presence with thanksgiving,
Let us shout joyfully to Him with psalms.
For the LORD is a great God
And a great King above all gods,
In whose hand are the depths of the earth,
The peaks of the mountains are His also.
The sea is His, for it was He who made it,
And His hands formed the dry land.

Come, let us worship and bow down,
Let us kneel before the LORD our maker.
For He is our God,
And we are the people of His pasture and the sheep of His hand.
Today, if you would hear His voice,
Do not harden your hearts, as at Meribah,
As in the day of Massah in the wilderness,
When your fathers tested Me,
They tried Me, though they had seen My work.
For forty years I loathed that generation,
And said they are a people who err in their heart,

And they do not know My ways.
Therefore I swore in My anger,
Truly they shall not enter into My rest.

OUR FATHER, we offer praise to You with this psalm,
  which begins with a joyful shout to the rock of our salvation—
  but ends with a somber warning.
The inspired psalmist moves from
      the joy of salvation,
      the love of thanksgiving,
      and the singing of praise
      (all celebrating the greatness of Your saving glory)
  to a threat of everlasting judgment—the forfeiture of eternal rest
    for those who stubbornly harden their hearts against You.

May we never be like those with Moses in the wilderness,
  who complained and put You to the test,
  even *after* they saw Your glory in an unparalleled display.[1]
Your Word shows us such a stark contrast between
  those who come to You in faith and those who refuse.
For the faithful, there will be permanent
  joy, hope, and blessing.
For the faithless, there is nothing to look forward to but
  hopelessness, judgment, and everlasting punishment.
Hold us by Your grace, that we may be counted
    with the faithful.

We thank You for Your precious grace in saving us, Lord.
You are both the source and the object of our highest joy.
We sing out to You because our hearts cannot contain

---

1. Numbers 14:1-35

the gladness of salvation, and in exalting You,
    we are lifted even higher.
You are our light and our salvation,
    the stronghold and sanctuary in whom we find refuge.[1]
You refresh our souls daily with joys
    we can neither fathom nor fully count.

We confess, however, with deep sadness,
    that we are rebellious by nature,
    so we do not always serve You as we should.
We want to bask in the fullness of Your joy
    and find our deepest delight in the sunshine of Your glory.
Yet we are prone to wander.
We are too easily tempted.
We are weak and worldly and wrong-hearted creatures,
    great debtors to Your mercy
        and in desperate need of Your grace.

And so, Lord, we thank You that You are faithful and just to forgive.[2]
We are prompted from hearts transformed at our salvation
    to run to You and embrace You with glad surrender.
Help us, Lord, to be earnest and honest in self-examination,[3]
    and in that exercise may Your Spirit
    testify together with our spirit
        that we are true children of our heavenly Father,[4]
        born again to a living hope.[5]
Grant us grace that the fruit of regeneration
    will flourish and multiply in our lives.
        May our tears be tears of true repentance;

---

1. Psalm 27:1
2. 1 John 1:9
3. 2 Corinthians 13:5
4. Romans 8:16; John 1:12
5. 1 Peter 1:3; 2 Corinthians 5:17

may our hope be grounded solely in Your Word;
may our works be energized by love;
and may our faith endure to the end of time!

We rest in the promise that none could ever snatch us
out of Your mighty hand.[1]
May we feel the firmness of Your grip on us,
and may we reflect the passion of Your love.
We ask these things humbly in the name of Christ. Amen.

1. John 10:28-29

LOVING WITH A HEAVENLY LOVE

1 John 4:7-19

Beloved, let us love one another, for love is from God; and everyone who loves is born of God and knows God. The one who does not love does not know God, for God is love. By this the love of God was manifested in us, that God has sent His only begotten Son into the world so that we might live through Him. In this is love, not that we loved God, but that He loved us and sent His Son to be the propitiation for our sins. Beloved, if God so loved us, we also ought to love one another. No one has seen God at any time; if we love one another, God abides in us, and His love is perfected in us. By this we know that we abide in Him and He in us, because He has given us of His Spirit. We have seen and testify that the Father has sent the Son to be the Savior of the world.

Whoever confesses that Jesus is the Son of God, God abides in him, and he in God. We have come to know and have believed the love which God has for us. God is love, and the one who abides in love abides in God, and God abides in him. By this, love is perfected with us, so that we may have confidence in the day of judgment; because as He is, so also are we in this world. There is no fear in love, but perfect love casts out fear, because fear involves punishment, and the one who fears is not perfected in love. We love, because He first loved us.

FATHER, Your love "has been poured out within our hearts
    through the Holy Spirit who was given to us,"[1]
    and we confess that the only reason we love at all
        is because You first loved us.
Your love enables us to love You and one another
    in a way that is beyond human capacity.
    Magnify that love in our hearts,
        and enlarge our hearts in the process.

We thank You for loving us into Your family and kingdom.
As we come before You now, fill us with that heavenly love
    so that our worship will be a foretaste of true heavenly praise.
Give us Christlike love for one another—
    the love that takes up towel and basin
        and gladly serves in the lowliest place.
Give us grace to render that service and sacrifice
    with overflowing joy and true humility.
Empower us to encourage and love one another
    and give of ourselves freely, just as Christ did for us.
May we see beyond the faces of those whom we serve—
    as blessed, beloved, and precious as they may be—
    and may we look to You, the One whom we are to love
        with all our heart, soul, mind, and strength.[2]
And so may we truly minister to one another *as unto the Lord.*[3]

Help us to love You more.
Free us from the grip of trivial worldly attractions
    that vie for our affections.
Show us in the process the vanity of our sins
    and the barrenness of this world's values,

---

1. Romans 5:5
2. Mark 12:30
3. Colossians 3:23

and cause us to fix our affections on heavenly things.[1]
May our daily walk thus bring us
    ever nearer to the cross and ever closer to heaven!

Spirit of God, write abiding truths on our hearts
    through our study of Your Word this day.
Nourish our souls with the food that is needful for us[2]—
    the food that endures to eternal life.[3]

We praise You and find our greatest joy and peace
    in Jesus' name. Amen.

---

1. Colossians 3:2
2. Proverbs 30:8
3. John 6:27

OVERFLOWING WITH GRATITUDE FOR GOD'S LOVE

PSALM 139:1-10

O LORD, You have searched me and known me.
  You know when I sit down and when I rise up;
You understand my thought from afar.
You scrutinize my path and my lying down,
And are intimately acquainted with all my ways.
Even before there is a word on my tongue,
Behold, O LORD, You know it all.
You have enclosed me behind and before,
And laid Your hand upon me.
Such knowledge is too wonderful for me;
It is too high, I cannot attain to it.

Where can I go from Your Spirit?
Or where can I flee from Your presence?
If I ascend to heaven, You are there;
If I make my bed in Sheol, behold, You are there.
If I take the wings of the dawn,
If I dwell in the remotest part of the sea,
Even there Your hand will lead me,
And Your right hand will lay hold of me.

HEAVENLY FATHER, it is such a staggering
        realization to understand that You,
        the infinite God of the universe, truly love us—
        with a love that is everlasting.
You set that love on us before time began.[1]
You chose us and ordained us to eternal life
        in timeless ages past,[2]
        and therefore we rest in the assurance
                that Your love will endure
                        into the countless ages of eternity future.

You have made us a chosen race,
        a royal priesthood, a holy nation, a people
                for Your own possession.
Open our mouths to proclaim Your excellency,
        because You have drawn us out of darkness
        and into the marvelous light of Your truth.[3]
You raised us up out of spiritual death
        through the saving truth of the gospel,
        and You made us fully alive in Christ by Your Spirit—
                all because of the great love
                        with which You loved us.[4]

We now have the blessed privilege of being not only
        Your dutiful slaves but also
                Your blessed sons and daughters.
We say with the apostle Paul,
        "Blessed be the God and Father of our Lord Jesus Christ,
        who has blessed us with every spiritual blessing
                in the heavenly places in Christ."[5]

1. Ephesians 1:4
2. Titus 1:1-2
3. 1 Peter 2:9
4. Ephesians 2:1-4
5. Ephesians 1:3

You richly provide us with good things to enjoy.[1]
Although in this world we face frequent
  tribulations,[2] sorrows, sickness, and suffering for Christ's sake,
   all the bitterness of life is sweetened by Your promises
    and held in check by Your merciful grace.
So many tokens of Your goodness and mercy encourage us
  amid the discouraging realities of life in this fallen world.
When we become downhearted,
  You give us sympathy and support in abundant measure.
When we face grave temptations,
  You are our Guardian and refuge.
  You strengthen us in the hour of trial;
  and in the wake of every victory
   You lead us in triumph.

Accept, O Lord, our feeble efforts to praise You and thank You.
You never cease to love us;
  You never fail to preserve us from the evil one;
  and You never skimp in showing us mercy.
You will never cast us away;
  Christ has promised never to leave us or forsake us;
  and Your Holy Spirit is with us—and in us—forever.[3]
You faithfully preserve Your saints eternally.[4]

Dear Lord of all mercy, remove from our hearts
  the festering pride, evil desire, false motives,
  insincerity, envy, longing for worldly prominence,
  and every other secret sin.
Help us to wait patiently upon You.
May we learn to see the wisdom of Your providence

---

1. 1 Timothy 6:17
2. John 16:33
3. John 14:16-17
4. Psalm 37:28

not only in Your actions, but also in Your delays.
Stir in our hearts a proper sense of awe and reverence
    for Your perfections,
        and may we learn to love and pursue holiness
            as befits children of the Holy One.
Inscribe Your love on our hearts
    in such a way that our every thought
        will somehow be a reflection of that love.

We celebrate Your grace and goodness to us
    in the covenant of salvation.
May we be a covenant-keeping people,
    as You are a covenant-keeping God.

We thank You that in Christ we have
        overcome the world,
        fulfilled the law,
        found justifying righteousness,
        seen death swallowed up in victory,
        and received all we need
    for everything You require of us.
To Your name alone we give glory,
    offering You our praise for Christ's sake. Amen.

CONTEMPLATING ETERNAL LIFE AND JOY

1 JOHN 5:1-13

Whoever believes that Jesus is the Christ is born of God, and whoever loves the Father loves the child born of Him. By this we know that we love the children of God, when we love God and observe His commandments. For this is the love of God, that we keep His commandments; and His commandments are not burdensome. For whatever is born of God overcomes the world; and this is the victory that has overcome the world—our faith.

Who is the one who overcomes the world, but he who believes that Jesus is the Son of God? This is the One who came by water and blood, Jesus Christ; not with the water only, but with the water and with the blood. It is the Spirit who testifies, because the Spirit is the truth. For there are three that testify: the Spirit and the water and the blood; and the three are in agreement. If we receive the testimony of men, the testimony of God is greater; for the testimony of God is this; that He has testified concerning His Son. The one who believes in the Son of God has the testimony in himself; the one who does not believe God has made Him a liar, because he has not believed in the testimony that God has given concerning His Son. And the testimony is this, that God has given us eternal life, and this life is in His Son. He who has the Son has the life; he who does not have the Son of God does not have the life.

These things I have written to you who believe in the name of the Son of God, so that you may know that you have eternal life.

FATHER, we thank You for the truth revealed in Your written Word,
    which testifies to us about Your Son,
        the Lord Jesus Christ.
We thank You also for the testimony of the Holy Spirit,
    who attested to Christ with many miracles and wonders
        at the dawn of the gospel era.
We thank You as well for the audible testimony You gave
    at the time of Jesus' water baptism:
    "This is My beloved Son, in whom I am well pleased."[1]
And above all, we thank You for the blood of Christ,
    the ultimate proof that Christ always does
        the things that are pleasing to You.[2]
That precious blood is a most satisfactory sacrifice
    for all the sins of all who would ever believe
        these testimonies about Christ.
We affirm that all these impeccable testimonies are true,
    and we confess that Christ is indeed
        the Son of God and the only Savior—
        and that by believing in Him we have eternal life.

We thank You, O God, that You granted us
    this eternal life through Your mercy.
One of the fruits of that gift for us is eternal joy.
What amazing love that You sent Your Son to
    sorrow, suffer, and die that we might know *joy*!
How can we thank You enough?

You have commanded us to rejoice always and in every circumstance—
    even our trials are an occasion for rejoicing.[3]
Joy is such a delightful duty,
    and yet we humbly confess that because we are weak and sinful,

---

1. Matthew 3:17
2. John 8:29
3. Philippians 4:4; 1 Thessalonians 5:16; James 1:2

grumbling and complaining sometimes seem to come more naturally
      as a response to the issues of life.
Forgive us for such a bleak and ungrateful response
    to the grace You show us each day,
    and help us even now to be glad participants in heaven's joy.

By making joy both a privilege and a duty in our daily lives,
    and by preparing us for an even greater eternal joy,
    You show Yourself to be a God of gladness and cheer.
Though sorrow is an inevitable part of the human experience
    because of our sin,
    You meet our sorrow with countless reasons
        to be grateful and glad,
        full of hope and full of rejoicing.
Our weeping may endure for a night,
    but joy will come in the morning.[1]

Your mercies, likewise, are new every morning.[2]
How gracious and merciful You are
    to those who are sinful and were once Your enemies![3]
We are utterly unworthy,
    but still You chose to bless us with so great a salvation.
You have turned our mourning into dancing;
    You loosed our sackcloth and clothed us with gladness.[4]
Even in our sorrow we find our way to joy by thinking of
      Your love,
      Your forgiveness,
      Your tender mercies,
      Your sympathy for our weaknesses,
    and the hope of eternity in Your presence.

---

1. Psalm 30:5
2. Lamentations 3:23
3. Romans 5:1,8-11
4. Psalm 30:11

We look forward with glad expectation
    to that perfect, endless joy that will be ours
        when we meet You face-to-face.

Fill our hearts even now with heaven, dearest Lord.
May we live free of the failures
    that mar our lives and spoil all earthly joy.
Lord, lead us out of those things
    into the place of obedience and faithfulness.
We thank You for the promises of
    Your power and Your care.
In the name of Christ our Savior we pray. Amen.

LIVING A LITTLE HEAVEN ON EARTH

Romans 5:1-11

Therefore, having been justified by faith, we have peace with God through our Lord Jesus Christ, through whom also we have obtained our introduction by faith into this grace in which we stand; and we exult in hope of the glory of God. And not only this, but we also exult in our tribulations, knowing that tribulation brings about perseverance; and perseverance, proven character; and proven character, hope; and hope does not disappoint, because the love of God has been poured out within our hearts through the Holy Spirit who was given to us.

For while we were still helpless, at the right time Christ died for the ungodly. For one will hardly die for a righteous man; though perhaps for the good man someone would dare even to die. But God demonstrates His own love toward us, in that while we were yet sinners, Christ died for us. Much more then, having now been justified by His blood, we shall be saved from the wrath of God through Him. For if while we were enemies we were reconciled to God through the death of His Son, much more, having been reconciled, we shall be saved by His life. And not only this, but we also exult in God through our Lord Jesus Christ, through whom we have now received the reconciliation.

FATHER, we are both emboldened and humbled
  when we consider how we have been justified by faith.

We have been introduced into Your matchless grace;
    we have been given a strong and secure standing before You.
And now we have every reason to rejoice
    in the hope of one day receiving unimaginable glory
        that we do not deserve,
          as joint heirs with Christ,
            to whom all glory rightfully belongs.
We thank You for pouring into our hearts divine love
    through the Holy Spirit.
How amazing it is that when we were helpless and ungodly,
    Christ shed His blood for us,
    not only saving us from Your just wrath
        but also reconciling us to Yourself
          as lost sons and daughters!

You chose us, called us, and redeemed us, O God,
    and You have accepted us in the Beloved[1]—
    Your only begotten Son, the Lord Jesus Christ,
    beloved by You with an eternal love that transcends
        every power, every force,
        every creature, and every measure
          of both time and eternity.
That love is the ultimate reason for our redemption.
We therefore owe Christ our most heartfelt love,
    highest honor, and deepest reverence.

And yet we confess with shame that our love for Him is
    too feeble, too fickle, too faithless
    to honor Him as He deserves.
We are too easily distracted, too easily discouraged,
    and too easily disturbed by the trials, temptations, and trivialities
        of daily life in this fallen world.

---

1. Ephesians 1:6

We are neither as poor in spirit nor as pure in heart[1] as we ought to be.
Forgive us for our arrogance
    and deeply-engrained self-love,
    and purge all such sins from our hearts.

One day we will love Christ perfectly.
One day we will serve Him more faithfully.
One day we will worship Him in true singleness of heart.
One day we will know Him as we ourselves are known by Him.
Now we see in a mirror dimly,
    but then we will see Him face-to-face,[2]
    and in so seeing Him, we shall be transformed—
    fully glorified, and instantly made to reflect His likeness[3]
        with that consummate perfection
            only Your grace can accomplish for us.

In the meantime, with all that our feeble hearts can muster,
    we worship the Lord Jesus;
    we seek to live in a way that continually expresses
        our thankfulness to Him;
    we seek to know Him better and serve Him
        ever more faithfully.
We ask You to make Him known through
    our words and our deeds to the needy souls around us.

We have found in Christ all our happiness and hope.
Grant us by grace the singleness of heart to keep
    our minds fixed on Him,
    our lives surrendered to Him,
    our words devoted to His honor,
    and our hands committed to His work.

---

1. Matthew 5:1-11
2. 1 Corinthians 13:12
3. 1 John 3:2

May the power of Your Spirit increase in us
    so that we might be more faithful witnesses for Christ
        in this hostile world—
    demonstrating the depth of His love,
    following the model of His self-sacrifice,
    walking in the footsteps of His example,
    conforming to the pattern of His self-sacrifice,
    reflecting the qualities of His character,
    bearing the marks of His sufferings,
    trusting in the efficacy of His death,
    living in the power of His resurrection,
    and declaring the trustworthiness of His truth
        as He Himself would proclaim it.

To know Christ is truly a foretaste of heaven's glory.
May we have a hunger to experience that heaven on earth
    in all its fullness,
        until we enter the great heaven of heavens
            and worship and serve our Lord and Savior
                with true perfection!

Forgive us, Father, for our daily failures and sins.
Help us to pursue Your righteousness more diligently each day
    in all that we do.
We pray these things in Jesus' name. Amen.

LIVING LIKE WE'RE REALLY AWAKE

ROMANS 13:8-14

O we nothing to anyone except to love one another; for he who loves his neighbor has fulfilled the law. For this, "You shall not commit adultery, you shall not murder, you shall not steal, you shall not covet," and if there is any other commandment, it is summed up in this saying, "You shall love your neighbor as yourself." Love does no wrong to a neighbor; therefore love is the fulfillment of the law.

Do this, knowing the time, that it is already the hour for you to awaken from sleep; for now salvation is nearer to us than when we believed. The night is almost gone, and the day is near. Therefore let us lay aside the deeds of darkness and put on the armor of light. Let us behave properly as in the day, not in carousing and drunkenness, not in sexual promiscuity and sensuality, not in strife and jealousy. But put on the Lord Jesus Christ, and make no provision for the flesh in regard to its lusts.

GRACIOUS FATHER, even Your law is an expression of your love. Not only does love perfectly fulfill the law's moral demands; it also powerfully testifies about the truth of the gospel.[1]

---

1. John 13:35

Our love for You
    and our love for one another
        furthermore demonstrate that we are spiritually awake
            to the soon return of Your Son,
            the Lord Jesus Christ, our Savior.

All the truths about You unveiled in Scripture, all the great doctrines,
    all aspects of the unfolding story of redemption come down to this:
        that we might know You,
        the only true God, through Jesus Christ,
        and walk in obedience to Him for our own eternal joy
        as a loving community of believers,
        bringing glory to Your holy name forever.[1]
Anyone who does not love does not truly know You,
    because You are a God of love.[2]
The sum of Your commandments is love.
All that you require of us is that we love You
    with all our heart, soul, mind, and strength,
    and love others as ourselves.[3]

And yet, Lord, we fall far short of loving You as we should.
Love for self too often overwhelms our love for one another.
Even the best of our love is but a faint glimmer
    of what it ought to be.
We stand in desperate need of daily grace and forgiveness,
    and we confess that apart from Your mercy to us
        we would be utterly without hope.
But when we were lost, You found us.
You called us and drew us to Christ.
You brought us up out of a horrible pit—
    out of the miry clay—and set our feet upon a rock.[4]

1. John 17:3-26
2. 1 John 4:8
3. Matthew 22:36-40
4. Psalm 40:2

We want to be spiritually awakened.
Help us to realize and bear in mind that our final salvation,
    the eternal glory of heaven,
      is nearer to us than when we believed.
The day will soon dawn when we enter
    the glory of Your presence.
Until that dawning, while we remain in this world
    before Your Son's glorious return,
      we yearn to live in holy, not sinful, ways.

Empower us unto holiness as we seek to walk in a way
    that is consistent with Your wonderful love and
      Your perfect righteousness.
Give us humility to know that no matter how we resolve
    to live to Your honor,
      we have no strength of our own to accomplish that end.
So we walk by faith from day to day,
    depending on our heavenly Father to meet our needs.
Grant us more of the faith that overcomes the world.[1]

It is our blessed privilege as Your children
    to come boldly to the throne of grace again and again,
where we always receive mercy and find grace to help
    in time of need.[2]
Christ paid an infinite price to cover our sins,
    and therefore the wellspring of Your mercy
      is free and inexhaustible.
Such is the great love You bestowed on us,
    even when we were dead in our trespasses.[3]

We come therefore to worship You
    as those who live by Your love.

---

1. 1 John 5:4
2. Hebrews 4:16
3. Ephesians 2:3-4

May Your love be the mold that shapes
    our actions, our words,
    our character, and our very lives.
May love be the rule by which we live,
    the principle that governs our dealings with others,
    and a signboard for the whole world to see and honor Christ.
We pray in His precious name. Amen.

WEEK 18

BASKING IN GOD'S LOVE

Ephesians 1:1-14

*P*aul, an apostle of Christ Jesus by the will of God, to the saints who are at Ephesus and who are faithful in Christ Jesus: Grace to you and peace from God our Father and the Lord Jesus Christ.

Blessed be the God and Father of our Lord Jesus Christ, who has blessed us with every spiritual blessing in the heavenly places in Christ, just as He chose us in Him before the foundation of the world, that we would be holy and blameless before Him. In love He predestined us to adoption as sons through Jesus Christ to Himself, according to the kind intention of His will, to the praise of the glory of His grace, which He freely bestowed on us in the Beloved. In Him we have redemption through His blood, the forgiveness of our trespasses, according to the riches of His grace which He lavished on us. In all wisdom and insight He made known to us the mystery of His will, according to His kind intention which He purposed in Him with a view to an administration suitable to the fullness of the times, that is, the summing up of all things in Christ, things in the heavens and things on the earth. In Him also we have obtained an inheritance, having been predestined according to His purpose who works all things after the counsel of His will, to the end that we who were the first to hope in Christ would be to the praise of His glory. In Him, you also, after listening to the message of truth, the gospel of your salvation—having also believed, you were sealed in Him with the Holy Spirit of promise, who is given as a pledge of our inheritance, with a view to the redemption of God's own possession, to the praise of His glory.

❉

FATHER, we come before You to echo and to celebrate
        the vast blessings of our redemption,
        to the praise of Your glory.

We rejoice that we have been blessed
        with every spiritual blessing in the heavenly places in Christ.
Before the foundation of the world,
        You chose us to be holy and blameless in Your presence.
We were lovingly predestined to become
        Your sons and daughters.
We have now obtained complete redemption
        through the blood of Christ.
His sacrifice on the cross purchased
        full forgiveness for all our sins.
Thus we have been lavished with Your grace,
        and You have opened the eyes of our understanding
                so that we might know the hope of Your calling.
You have given us an immeasurable inheritance.[1]
And You have sealed all these promises
        by giving us Your Holy Spirit.

Before You even created the universe,
        it was Your eternal purpose to bestow on us
                Your love and Your grace,
        so that we might in turn worship Your Son forever
                with our love and our praise.
We get a small taste of that privilege now
        when we commune with You in prayer.

And so we acknowledge with deepest gratitude
        that we are the recipients of vast heavenly blessings.

---

1. Ephesians 1:18

You have deluged us with Your grace.
You have made us Your sons and daughters—
    even though we were Your avowed enemies.
We were dead and You gave us life.
We were in darkness and You brought us into the light.
We were separated from Christ,
    alienated from the commonwealth of Israel
        and strangers to the covenants of promise,
        having no hope and without God in the world.
We were far off, but You brought us near by the blood of Christ.[1]

Even now we stand in need of Your grace moment by moment.
Help us to abide in Christ and draw life and vitality
    as branches from the eternal Vine.
We know that we can do nothing good or holy
    without the strength He supplies.[2]
We desire to be fruitful and thus prove
    to be true and faithful disciples.[3]
We long to be bright beacons of Your truth in a world of darkness.
We earnestly hunger and thirst for Your righteousness.
Grant us the wisdom, the will, and the power
    to work for what pleases You.[4]

Lord, we come before You eager to offer You our praise,
    but we confess that we are restrained by our inability to apprehend
        the greatness of Your glory and Your grace toward us.
We can't even discern our own errors rightly.
Acquit us of hidden faults;
    keep us back from presumptuous sins.[5]

---

1. Ephesians 2:12-13
2. John 15:5
3. John 15:8
4. Philippians 2:13
5. Psalm 19:12-13

Liberate us, we pray, from all the limitations of our fallen sinfulness
and set us free to praise You with full understanding.

Be honored as we bow our hearts before You in prayer,
and be glorified once more as we raise our voices
before You in worship.
Fix our thoughts on Your truth and give us singleness of mind
so that our worship may be acceptable to You.
We earnestly desire these things in the name of Christ. Amen.

THE ACHING HEART SATISFIED IN CHRIST

2 Corinthians 3

A re we beginning to commend ourselves again? Or do we need, as some, letters of commendation to you or from you? You are our letter, written in our hearts, known and read by all men; being manifested that you are a letter of Christ, cared for by us, written not with ink but with the Spirit of the living God, not on tablets of stone but on tablets of human hearts.

Such confidence we have through Christ toward God. Not that we are adequate in ourselves to consider anything as coming from ourselves, but our adequacy is from God, who also made us adequate as servants of a new covenant, not of the letter but of the Spirit; for the letter kills, but the Spirit gives life.

But if the ministry of death, in letters engraved on stones, came with glory, so that the sons of Israel could not look intently at the face of Moses because of the glory of his face, fading as it was, how will the ministry of the Spirit fail to be even more with glory? For if the ministry of condemnation has glory, much more does the ministry of righteousness abound in glory. For indeed what had glory, in this case has no glory because of the glory that surpasses it. For if that which fades away was with glory, much more that which remains is in glory.

Therefore having such a hope, we use great boldness in our speech, and are not like Moses, who used to put a veil over his face so that the sons of Israel would not look intently at the end of what was fading away. But their minds were hardened; for until this very day at the reading of the old

*covenant the same veil remains unlifted, because it is removed in Christ. But
to this day whenever Moses is read, a veil lies over their heart; but whenever
a person turns to the Lord, the veil is taken away. Now the Lord is the Spirit,
and where the Spirit of the Lord is, there is liberty. But we all, with unveiled
face, beholding as in a mirror the glory of the Lord, are being transformed
into the same image from glory to glory, just as from the Lord, the Spirit.*

ALMIGHTY GOD, Your judgments are unsearchable
    and Your ways unfathomable;
    from You and through You and to You are all things.[1]
We are not sufficient in ourselves
    to claim anything as coming from us.
Our only adequacy is what we receive from Your gracious hand.
You created us; not we ourselves.
By Your grace alone we are Your people
    and the sheep of Your pasture.[2]
You have made us partakers in a glorious New Covenant.
In Jesus Christ we can see the unveiled brightness
        of Your glory face-to-face.[3]
We are therefore participants in the ministry of righteousness,
    and living reflections of that glory which does not fade away.

All the tainted glory of this fallen world is fading away.
We rejoice in that knowledge,
    and we look forward to the coming of Your kingdom,
        when the glory of Christ will shine brightly
            throughout all the earth.
In the meantime, we earnestly desire to be vessels of His glory,

---

1. Romans 11:33,36
2. Psalm 100:3
3. 2 Corinthians 4:6

reflecting the beauty of His moral perfection
and establishing the honor of His name
so that all the world may see and hear.

Yet we know, Lord, that sin has blinded the minds
of those who do not know Christ.
A veil has been erected that obscures eternal truth
from the hearts of so many.
Make us a living letter—not with ink and paper
but by the Spirit of the Living God—
to be known and read by all,
so that the ministry of righteousness
may truly abound in glory.

We grieve over the heartache caused by sin.
We know that the consequences of evildoing are always bitter.
Although temptation invariably comes to us
with promises of ease, comfort, pleasure, and self-gratification,
we have learned the hard way that every fruit of evil
is thoroughly and inevitably corrupt.
We know from the testimony of Your Word
that sin is what unleashed pain and suffering
into the universe in the first place.
Help us to be mindful of that when we are tempted,
and help us to hate sin
even more than we despise sin's consequences.

How our hearts rejoice that Christ has been manifested
to put away sin by the sacrifice of Himself.[1]
He satisfies the longing soul
and fills the hungry soul with goodness.[2]
He delivers our souls from death

1. Hebrews 9:26
2. Psalm 107:9

and He keeps our feet from stumbling
      so that we might walk before You in the light of life.[1]

He is the One who said,
      "All things have been handed over to Me by My Father;
      and no one knows the Son except the Father;
      nor does anyone know the Father except the Son,
      and anyone to whom the Son wills to reveal Him.
            Come to Me, all who are weary and heavy laden,
                  and I will give you rest.
            Take My yoke upon you and learn from Me,
            for I am gentle and humble in heart,
            and you will find rest for your souls.
            For My yoke is easy and My burden is light."[2]
Only He can salve all the pains of our hearts
      and satisfy the deepest longings of our souls.

That is why, dear Father,
      we come to worship You in Jesus' name.
By Him we have obtained access into Your presence.
Because of His sacrifice on our behalf,
      we have received full pardon for all our sins.
We come clothed in the spotless garment
      of His perfect righteousness.

Nevertheless, we come with a deep sense of spiritual poverty,
      marveling that we can be so loved and lavished with such grace
      when we are so often forgetful of Your goodness
            and so prone to self-indulgence.
Lord, we thank You for that endless forgiveness that comes to us,
      and we praise You for having prepared for us
            a glorious eternal destiny.

1. Psalm 56:13
2. Matthew 11:27-30

We trust You fully for the grace needed
>   to sustain us until our dying day
>   or until that day when we meet the Lord in the air
>   to be with Him forevermore.[1]
Hear our prayer, Father, for we offer it according to Your will
>   and in Your Son's precious name. Amen.

---

1. 1 Thessalonians 4:16-18; John 14:1-3

WEEK 20

THANKING GOD FOR
A SPIRITUAL BANQUET

JAMES 1:17-27

Every good thing given and every perfect gift is from above, coming down from the Father of lights, with whom there is no variation or shifting shadow. In the exercise of His will He brought us forth by the word of truth, so that we would be a kind of first fruits among His creatures.

This you know, my beloved brethren. But everyone must be quick to hear, slow to speak and slow to anger; for the anger of man does not achieve the righteousness of God. Therefore, putting aside all filthiness and all that remains of wickedness, in humility receive the word implanted, which is able to save your souls. But prove yourselves doers of the word, and not merely hearers who delude themselves. For if anyone is a hearer of the word and not a doer, he is like a man who looks at his natural face in a mirror; for once he has looked at himself and gone away, he has immediately forgotten what kind of person he was. But one who looks intently at the perfect law, the law of liberty, and abides by it, not having become a forgetful hearer but an effectual doer, this man will be blessed in what he does.

If anyone thinks himself to be religious, and yet does not bridle his tongue but deceives his own heart, this man's religion is worthless. Pure and undefiled religion in the sight of our God and Father is this: to visit orphans and widows in their distress, and to keep oneself unstained by the world.

101

PRECIOUS FATHER IN HEAVEN, we gratefully
  acknowledge that
    every perfect gift and every good thing
      we have ever received is from You,
      the Father of heavenly lights.
We confess that we do not deserve any good thing at all from You,
    so we can only stand in humble gratitude
      that You have given us so precious a gift
        as eternal life in Christ.
In the exercise of Your sovereign will
    and in accord with Your eternal good pleasure,
You brought us forth out of spiritual death through Your Word,
    that imperishable seed by which we are born again
      to a living hope.[1]

Human language does not contain words
    sufficient to express our thankfulness
      for the salvation You have wrought in us.
When we think of the magnitude of Your mercy
    and the immensity of the grace You have bestowed on us,
    we earnestly desire to be doers of the Word,
    living emblems of the perfect righteousness
      and overflowing grace to which we owe everything.

And yet, Lord, we sorrowfully acknowledge our stubborn sinfulness
    and the desperate wickedness that remains in our hearts
      and continually causes us to sin
      against that inexhaustible grace
        to which we owe everything.
Endow us with the power and the will
    to lay aside what remains of our sin
      and humbly receive the engrafted Word
        that is able to save us.

---

1. 1 Peter 1:23

Graciously equip us to cleanse our hands,
    purify our hearts,[1]
    mortify the deeds of our flesh,[2]
    cast off the works of darkness,
  and put on the armor of light.[3]

Those are all things that are pleasing in Your sight,
  and therefore we know You will grant the request.
In fact, Your beauty is on display for all to see
  in Your goodness and graciousness to us as unworthy sinners.
We are awed by the promise to all who trust in You through Christ
  that all things are ours[4] and that Your divine power
    has granted to us everything pertaining to life and godliness.[5]

Because You are for us, we know that no one can be against us.
Because You justify us, no accuser can condemn us.
Your own Son, the Lord Jesus Christ—
    having died for our sin,
    risen from the grave,
    and ascended into heaven—
  secures us and is even now at the right hand of Your throne,
  interceding for us.[6]

We praise You, Lord, for these precious promises
  that nourish and gladden our souls with infinite comfort.
We fall back on such words of hope in times of need and sorrow,
  humbly acknowledging Your faithfulness
    with profound gratitude.

Meanwhile, it is to our own deep shame

---

1. James 4:8
2. Romans 8:13
3. Romans 13:12
4. 1 Corinthians 3:21-23
5. 2 Peter 1:3-4
6. Romans 8:31-34

that we are fickle and untrustworthy.
We know that even when we are faithless, You abide faithful.[1]
    Your mercies are new every morning.[2]
But help us to lay hold of Your promises not merely for comfort and hope
    but also as motivation, encouragement, edification,
        and an example to follow
            as we seek more earnestly to be faithful.

We thank You that nothing can ever separate us from Your love—
    revealed in Christ, your Son,
    and shed abroad in our hearts by the Holy Spirit.[3]
You have spread before us an abundant table full of good things—
    more blessings than we could ever know or imagine!
Cleanse us before we feast at Your banquet,
    so that nothing may hinder the worship
        we offer You now in prayer.
We ask these things in the name
    of Him who was delivered up for our sins,
    the Lord Jesus Christ. Amen.

---

1. 2 Timothy 2:13
2. Lamentations 3:21
3. Romans 8:35; 5:5

WAITING PATIENTLY FOR GOD'S PERFECT JUSTICE

James 5:1-11

Come now, you rich, weep and howl for your miseries which are coming upon you. Your riches have rotted and your garments have become moth-eaten. Your gold and your silver have rusted; and their rust will be a witness against you and will consume your flesh like fire. It is in the last days that you have stored up your treasure! Behold, the pay of the laborers who mowed your fields, and which has been withheld by you, cries out against you; and the outcry of those who did the harvesting has reached the ears of the Lord of Sabaoth. You have lived luxuriously on the earth and led a life of wanton pleasure; you have fattened your hearts in a day of slaughter. You have condemned and put to death the righteous man; he does not resist you.

Therefore be patient, brethren, until the coming of the Lord. The farmer waits for the precious produce of the soil, being patient about it, until it gets the early and late rains. You too be patient; strengthen your hearts, for the coming of the Lord is near. Do not complain, brethren, against one another, so that you yourselves may not be judged; behold, the Judge is standing right at the door. As an example, brethren, of suffering and patience, take the prophets who spoke in the name of the Lord. We count those blessed who endured. You have heard of the endurance of Job and have seen the outcome of the Lord's dealings, that the Lord is full of compassion and is merciful.

GRACIOUS FATHER of mercies and God of all comfort,[1]
    the Lord Jesus said that in this world
        we would have tribulation.[2]
Indeed, all who desire to live godly in Christ Jesus
    will be persecuted.[3]
A slave is not greater than his master,
    and because the world persecuted Christ,
        it is by no means a marvel that worldly hearts today
            still hate and revile those who stand faithfully
                for the truth He proclaims.[4]

Yet we know that Christ has already overcome the world.
We know that His coming in glory
    draws closer with each passing moment.
We know that the prophets and redeemed people of old
    were blessed through the things they suffered.
We remember especially the outcome of Job's trials.
We know that the righteous suffer
    and sinners prosper only temporarily.
We know that no trouble can assault us
    without Your express permission.[5]
Meanwhile, You uphold us with sufficient grace
    to endure every tribulation,
    and You make for us a way of escape from every temptation.[6]

May we draw patience, courage, and strength from that knowledge.
Energize our hearts unto godliness,
    even as You humble us through our trials.

---

1. 2 Corinthians 1:3
2. John 16:33
3. 2 Timothy 3:12
4. John 15:18-20
5. Cf. Job 1:9-12; 2:1-7; Luke 22:31
6. 1 Corinthians 10:13

We know that a day of justice is coming,
>	when the Lord Jesus will be revealed from heaven
>	>	with His mighty angels in flaming fire,
>	>	to deal out retribution to all
>	>	>	who do not obey the gospel.[1]

So enemies of the gospel—
>	including all who are prosperous in this life
>	>	but poor toward You—
>	have nothing to look forward to in eternity
>	>	but judgment.

Everything they have ever gained will be eternally lost.
As for us, we will behold Your face in righteousness.
We will be satisfied when we awaken,
>	transformed into living images of Christ.[2]

And on top of that,
>	You have elevated us as Your own sons and daughters
>	>	and made us joint heirs with the Lord Jesus,
>	to whom all glory belongs—if indeed we suffer with Him
>	>	so that we may also be glorified with Him.[3]

So Father, we come as humble and undeserving sinners to worship You,
>	the Most High God, righteous Judge,
>	Father of glory, Creator and sovereign of the universe.

You are great and greatly to be praised.
Your greatness is unsearchable.[4]
>	You are abundant in power;
>	Your wisdom is beyond measure.

You lift up the humble and cast the wicked down.[5]

---

1. 2 Thessalonians 1:5-10
2. Psalm 17:15; 1 John 3:2
3. Romans 8:17
4. Psalm 145:3
5. Psalm 147:5-6

We bless You for the gospel of peace
    that delivered our souls from the lowest hell.[1]
Thank You for the peace that prevails through the gospel:
        peace with You,
        peace with one another,
        and peace in our hearts.

Still, we stand in desperate need of Your mercy
    with every breath we draw.
Our hearts are prone to be faltering and unfaithful.
Deliver us from the temptations of this world,
    the deceits of false religion,
    the errors of our own ignorance,
    the weakness of our fallen flesh,
    and the wiles of the devil.
Wash us from our daily sins so that we may worship You
    with pure hands and a clean heart.[2]
In the name of our Lord Jesus Christ we pray. Amen.

---

1. Psalm 86:13
2. Psalm 24:3-6

APPROACHING GOD
WHEN DISMAYED

Psalms 42–43

As the deer pants for the water brooks,
  So my soul pants for You, O God.
My soul thirsts for God, for the living God;
When shall I come and appear before God?
My tears have been my food day and night,
While they say to me all day long, "Where is your God?"
These things I remember and I pour out my soul within me.
For I used to go along with the throng and lead
    them in procession to the house of God,
With the voice of joy and thanksgiving, a multitude
    keeping festival.

Why are you in despair, O my soul?
And why have you become disturbed within me?
Hope in God, for I shall again praise Him
For the help of His presence.
Oh my God, my soul is in despair within me;
Therefore I remember You from the land of the Jordan
And the peaks of Hermon, from Mount Mizar.
Deep calls to deep at the sound of Your waterfalls;
All Your breakers and Your waves have rolled over me.
The Lord will command His lovingkindness in the daytime;
And His song will be with me in the night,
A prayer to the God of my life.

I will say to God my rock, "Why have You forgotten me?
Why do I go mourning because of the oppression of the enemy?"
As a shattering of my bones, my adversaries revile me,
While they say to me all day long, "Where is your God?"
Why are you in despair, O my soul?
And why have you become disturbed within me?
Hope in God, for I shall yet praise Him,
The help of my countenance and my God.

Vindicate me, O God, and plead my case against an ungodly nation;
O deliver me from the deceitful and unjust man!
For You are the God of my strength; why have You rejected me?
Why do I go mourning because of the oppression of the enemy?

O send out Your light and Your truth, let them lead me;
Let them bring me to Your holy hill
And to Your dwelling places.
Then I will go to the altar of God,
To God my exceeding joy;
And upon the lyre I shall praise You, O God, my God.

Why are you in despair, O my soul?
And why are you disturbed within me?
Hope in God, for I shall again praise Him,
The help of my countenance and my God.

OUR FATHER, life in this sin-cursed world
   sometimes seems full of anguish—
   and we are too prone to fatigue and discouragement.
Sometimes we can only groan inwardly,
   echoing the sigh of all creation in this fallen realm.[1]

---

1. Romans 8:22-23

We desperately need the help and comfort of Your Holy Spirit
> to endure the ravages of sin amid the trials of daily life.

Often we don't even know how to pray,
>> but He makes intercession for us with groanings of His own
>>> that are too deep for human words.

And His prayers, unlike our feeble efforts
> to express the agony of our hearts,
>> are always in accord with Your perfect will.[1]

As Your children, we thirst for You and trust in You deep down.

We long to sense Your presence.

We need Your tender mercy.

We crave Your heavenly comfort.

We stand in awe of Your wisdom,
>> Your faithfulness,
>>> and Your perfect timing.

Our experience confirms the testimony of Your Word:
> You have never forsaken us.

Thus with settled confidence
> we echo the bold expectancy of the psalmist:
>> We shall yet praise You.

Bearing in mind those precious truths,
> we approach Your throne once again
>> with both fearful trembling and holy boldness.

You are both glorious and merciful;
> almighty and full of compassion;
>> a righteous Judge but extravagant with tender mercies.

We seek Your blessed favor in our times of need,
> although we know we are unworthy,
> because You have summoned us
>> to come confidently to the throne of grace.[2]

---

1. Romans 8:26-27
2. Hebrews 4:14-16

We are vile, fallen creatures, and Your glory is above the heavens.[1]
We are guilty but You are gracious.
We are weak but You are strong.
We are needy but You are rich in lovingkindness.
We are defiled by sin but You are spotlessly holy.
We are without merit, but You cover us
    with Your own perfect righteousness.
Most gladly, therefore, do we boast about our weaknesses,
    so that the power of Christ may dwell in us.
Help us to be content with weaknesses,
        with insults, with distresses, with persecutions,
            and with difficulties for Christ's sake.
Because when we are weak, then we are strong.[2]

By faith we have been made dead to sin
    and alive in Your holy presence.
You have blessed us with love—
        the likes of which we have never before known—
            love for You and love for one another.
You have showered us with grace and glory;
        no good thing have You withheld.[3]
You have brought us into the fellowship of the church,
    and you have supplied us everything
        that pertains to life and godliness.[4]

Use us to advance Your kingdom and bring honor to Your name!
Cleanse us from everything
    that would hinder us in accomplishing Your will,
    and receive our earnest prayers and worship
        in the name of Christ. Amen.

1. Psalm 113:4
2. 2 Corinthians 12:9-10
3. Psalm 84:11
4. 2 Peter 1:3

PRAYERS ON THE CROSS AND THE GOSPEL

CLINGING TO THE CROSS OF CHRIST

Psalm 118:14-29

The Lord is my strength and song,
  And He has become my salvation.
The sound of joyful shouting and salvation is in the tents
    of the righteous;
The right hand of the Lord does valiantly.
The right hand of the Lord is exalted;
The right hand of the Lord does valiantly.
I will not die, but live,
And tell of the works of the Lord.
The Lord has disciplined me severely,
But He has not given me over to death.

Open to me the gates of righteousness;
I shall enter through them, I shall give thanks to the Lord.
This is the gate of the Lord;
The righteous will enter through it.
I shall give thanks to You, for You have answered me,
And You have become my salvation.

The stone which the builders rejected
Has become the chief corner stone.
This is the Lord's doing;
It is marvelous in our eyes.

This is the day which the LORD has made;
Let us rejoice and be glad in it.
O LORD, do save, we beseech You;
O LORD, we beseech You, do send prosperity!
Blessed is the one who comes in the name of the LORD;
We have blessed you from the house of the LORD.
The LORD is God, and He has given us light;
Bind the festival sacrifice with cords to the horns of the altar.
You are my God, and I give thanks to You.
You are my God, I extol You.
Give thanks to the LORD, for He is good;
For His lovingkindness is everlasting.

DEAR GOD AND HEAVENLY FATHER,

You are our Deliverer, our shield and our refuge,
  the horn of our salvation.[1]
We praise You and offer our everlasting thankfulness
  because You sent Your son,
    the Lord Jesus Christ,
  to offer His life for our sake on the cross.
He is our strength and our song,
  and He has become our salvation.
Thus the stone that the builders rejected
  has become the cornerstone of our salvation[2]
    and the Savior of the world[3]—
    for no one in this world will ever find salvation
        in any other,
      nor can anyone come to You, Father, except through Him.[4]

---

1. Psalm 18:2
2. Matthew 21:42; Acts 4:11; Ephesians 2:20
3. 1 John 4:14
4. John 14:6

We add our own personal testimony to what Your Word declares:
    In the consummation of all things,
        those who have trusted in Christ will not be dismayed.[1]

We acknowledge, gracious Father, that our salvation is all Your work.
We are utterly helpless to save ourselves
    or contribute any merit of our own toward gaining Your favor.
But You took the initiative; You made the overture;
    You reconciled us to Yourself through Christ.
You made Him who had no sin to be sin for us,
    so that we might become the righteousness of God in Him.[2]
You, the offended party, acted first on our behalf
        while we were still enemies.[3]

We were willfully rebellious.
    Our appetites were evil.
    Our conduct was contrary to Your law.
    Our hearts were occupied with unworthy thoughts.
    Our motives were self-serving.
    Our attitudes were arrogant and smug.
    Our minds were hostile to You.
    We refused to submit to Your authority.
    We were hopelessly in bondage to sin
        and therefore unable to serve You as we ought.[4]
In all those ways we proved ourselves to be enemies
    of everything holy.

But You sent Your Son to redeem us from that bondage.
He purchased us from the slave-house of sin
    by offering Himself as a Substitute.
He took our place and carried our guilt to the cross.

---

1. Isaiah 28:16
2. 2 Corinthians 5:18-21
3. Romans 5:10
4. Romans 8:7-8

He bore for our sakes the just punishment of sin.

Now we are slaves of righteousness,[1] and it is our delightful duty
    to embrace Christ wholeheartedly as our rightful Master.
He is not only our Lord to rule over us.
He is also our Messiah and Deliverer;
        our Rabbi and Teacher;
        our Shepherd and Caretaker;
        our Great High Priest and Intercessor;
        and the spotless Lamb of God
    who made everlasting atonement once for all.[2]
He thus put away our sins forever by the sacrifice of Himself.[3]

We embrace Him alone as our Savior,
    trusting His work as fully sufficient.
We forego any effort to gain our own righteousness,
        supplement the work of Christ,
        earn fresh merit in Your eyes,
        or fit ourselves for heaven through our own efforts.[4]
We thus come by faith to the One who
    has already done everything for us—and even in that,
    we know that the only hope we have of abiding in Christ
        lies in the grace that made us alive to Him in the first place.[5]

And so we cling with penitent faith,
    asking that You keep us always near the cross.
In the name of the One crucified there we pray. Amen.

---

1. Romans 6:18
2. Hebrews 10:10
3. Hebrews 9:26-28
4. Philippians 3:7-11
5. Ephesians 2:8-10

UPHOLDING THE GOSPEL

Psalm 18:1-11

I love you, O Lord, my strength.
The Lord is my rock and my fortress and my deliverer,
My God, my rock, in whom I take refuge;
My shield and the horn of my salvation, my stronghold.
I call upon the Lord, who is worthy to be praised,
And I am saved from my enemies.

The cords of death encompassed me,
And the torrents of ungodliness terrified me.
The cords of Sheol surrounded me;
The snares of death confronted me.
In my distress I called upon the Lord,
And cried to my God for help;
He heard my voice out of His temple,
And my cry for help before Him came into His ears.

Then the earth shook and quaked;
And the foundations of the mountains were trembling
And were shaken, because He was angry.
Smoke went up out of His nostrils,
And fire from His mouth devoured;
Coals were kindled by it.

He bowed the heavens also, and came down
With thick darkness under His feet.
He rode upon a cherub and flew;
And He sped upon the wings of the wind.
He made darkness His hiding place, His canopy around Him,
Darkness of waters, thick clouds of skies.

WE LOVE YOU, O Lord, our strength.
You are all glorious, all powerful, all knowing,
    all wise, all gracious, and all sufficient.
You are the Alpha and Omega,
    the first and the last, the beginning and the end.[1]
All glory, honor, and power belong to You,
    and You alone are worthy to be praised;
    because You created all things,
    and because of Your will and for Your sake
        they were created.[2]

All knowledge belongs to You.
All wisdom originates with you.
No one ever gave You direction or counsel;
    no one ever instructed You in the way of understanding.
Humanity is like a drop from a bucket and a speck of dust on the scales.
All the nations are nothing before You—
    less than nothing. Meaningless.
No one and nothing compares to You.[3]

Yet You hold our eternal souls securely in Your loving hand.[4]

1. Revelation 22:13
2. Revelation 4:11
3. Isaiah 40:13-18
4. Titus 3:4-7

Because You are greater
> than all the enemies of righteousness combined,
> no one can ever snatch us away
>> from that place of tender care and safe-keeping.[1]

You are infinitely able to guard
> what we have committed to Your custody.[2]

We did nothing to earn the salvation You graciously provided for us.
And nothing we could ever do will forfeit that salvation,
> because we ourselves are graciously kept by Your power
>> through faith unto salvation,
>>> which is ready to be revealed in the last time.[3]

You gird us with strength and make our way blameless.[4]
You, the only wise God our Savior,
> are the One who keeps us from falling.
You will one day present us faultless
> before the presence of Your glory with exceeding joy.
All glory and majesty, dominion and power
> therefore belong to You alone, both now and forever.[5]

These truths powerfully remind us what helpless debtors we are
> to Your lovingkindness and rich grace.
Guard our hearts from idols;[6]
> give us the will and the energy to flee from all forms of idolatry.[7]

We know that some do desert the grace of Christ
> "for a different gospel."[8]
They were never true believers in the first place.

---

1. John 10:29
2. 2 Timothy 1:12
3. 1 Peter 1:5
4. Psalm 18:32
5. Jude 24-25
6. 1 John 5:21
7. 1 Corinthians 10:14
8. Galatians 1:6-10

They were false disciples who went out from us—
>   though they were not really of us;
>   for if they had been of us,
>   they would have remained with us.
But they went out, so that it would be shown
>   that they all are not of us.[1]

This is not unique to our age.
All through the centuries, legions of false disciples
>   have devised numerous counterfeit gospels—
>   damnable distortions of the truth,
>   carefully devised by the powers of darkness,
>   and clever enough, if possible, to deceive even the elect.[2]
We know that all who propagate such perversions are cursed.
Equip us to defend the true faith in the face of every false doctrine.

We celebrate Your goodness, Lord,
>   and we praise You for Your grace toward us,
>   confessing that we are completely unworthy of such favor.
We are overwhelmed when we contemplate our iniquities and failures,
>   knowing we fall far short
>   of that righteousness with which we have been covered:
>   the righteousness of Christ credited to our account.[3]
That is why we come before You now:
>   to worship You, to proclaim Your truth,
>   to sing Your praises, to be confronted by Your Word,
>   and to be conformed to the image of Christ,
>   in whose name we pray. Amen.

---

1. 1 John 2:19
2. Matthew 24:24
3. Romans 3:21-26; 4:3-5,22-24

WEEK 25

BEING DELIVERED FROM DARKNESS TO LIGHT

Colossians 1:1-18

*P*aul, an apostle of Jesus Christ by the will of God, and Timothy our *brother, to the saints and faithful brethren in Christ who are at Colossae: Grace to you and peace from God our Father.*

We give thanks to God, the Father of our Lord Jesus Christ, praying always for you, since we heard of your faith in Christ Jesus and the love which you have for all the saints; because of the hope laid up for you in heaven, of which you previously heard in the word of truth, the gospel which has come to you, just as in all the world also it is constantly bearing fruit and increasing, even as it has been doing in you also since the day you heard of it and understood the grace of God in truth; just as you learned it from Epaphras, our beloved fellow bond-servant, who is a faithful servant of Christ on our behalf, and he also informed us of your love in the Spirit.

For this reason also, since the day we heard of it, we have not ceased to pray for you and to ask that you may be filled with the knowledge of His will in all spiritual wisdom and understanding, so that you will walk in a manner worthy of the Lord, to please Him in all respects, bearing fruit in every good work and increasing in the knowledge of God; strengthened with all power, according to His glorious might, for the attaining of all steadfastness and patience; joyously giving thanks to the Father, who has qualified us to share in the inheritance of the saints in Light. For He rescued us from the domain of darkness, and transferred us to the kingdom of His beloved Son, in whom we have redemption, the forgiveness of sins.

*He is the image of the invisible God, the firstborn of all creation. For by
Him all things were created, both in the heavens and on earth, visible and
invisible, whether thrones or dominions or rulers or authorities—all things
have been created through Him and for Him. He is before all things, and in
Him all things hold together. He is also head of the body, the church; and He
is the beginning, the firstborn from the dead, so that He Himself will come
to have first place in everything.*

DEAR FATHER, this is the great glory of the gospel:
    that through Your beloved Son's work on the cross
        You rescue us from the domain of darkness
            and translate us into His kingdom of heavenly light,
            making us fit to share in the inheritance of the saints.

One of the most striking examples of that in Your Word
    is the testimony of the apostle Paul,
    who became a powerful advocate of the faith
        he once tried to destroy.[1]
All who believe can likewise testify
    that You have ransomed us from the bondage of sin,
    given us new life,
    and fully equipped us for Your service—
        even though like Saul of Tarsus,
        we were once blasphemers and disobedient.
We honor Your name because of Your transforming power in our lives.
You have put a new song in our mouths,
    a song of perpetual praise to You.[2]

We thank You for the work of the indwelling Holy Spirit,
    who transforms lives from the inside out.

---

1. Galatians 1:13-24
2. Psalm 40:3

We rejoice in the assurance that our sins are forgiven.

We are profoundly aware of our eternal indebtedness to Christ,
    who paid an incomprehensible price to set us free.

And we know that we are now free indeed[1]—
    free from enslavement to the law,
    and blessedly liberated from bondage to sin.

Enable us, we pray, to stand firm in that freedom.

Safeguard our hearts and seal our deliverance,
    so that we shall never again be subject to any yoke[2]
        other than the easy yoke and light burden of Christ.[3]

We know that apart from Your gracious empowerment,
    all our attempts at godly love and faithful service
        are utterly futile.

Apart from the Holy Spirit's enablement,
    we neither could nor would honor Jesus as Lord.[4]

Apart from the intercessory work of Christ,
    we know that we would falter.

Apart from the grace You give us to persevere,
    we would surely fall away.

And apart from the purifying power of Your Word,
    we could never be fit for heaven.[5]

We confess to our deep shame
    that our hearts are prone to coldness.

Our love for You is too shallow and too fickle
    to honor You in a worthy manner.

Our submission to Christ too often proves fragile and erratic.

Our walk is faltering and inconsistent.

---

1. John 8:36
2. Galatians 5:1
3. Matthew 11:30
4. 1 Corinthians 12:3
5. John 15:3; Hebrews 12:14

We are too susceptible
    to the lure of the world,
    the lusts of our own flesh,
    and the wiles of the devil.

Grant us more grace
    to be diligent in our duties,
    faithful in our devotion to Christ,
    industrious in the work of the gospel,
    clear in our testimony to the world,
    steadfast in our defense of the truth,
    and untiring in our service to You.
May all our conduct be worthy of the gospel of Christ.[1]
May every aspect of our lives bring honor to our Savior,
    our Lord Jesus Christ, in whose name we pray. Amen.

---

1. Philippians 1:27

PRAISING GOD FOR HOW HE HAS REVEALED HIMSELF

Hebrews 10:1-14

The Law, since it has only a shadow of the good things to come and not the very form of things, can never, by the same sacrifices which they offer continually year by year, make perfect those who draw near. Otherwise, would they not have ceased to be offered, because the worshipers, having once been cleansed, would no longer have had consciousness of sins? But in those sacrifices there is a reminder of sins year by year. For it is impossible for the blood of bulls and goats to take away sins. Therefore, when He comes into the world, He says, "Sacrifice and offering You have not desired, but a body You have prepared for Me; in whole burnt offerings and sacrifices for sin You have taken no pleasure." Then I said, "Behold, I have come (in the scroll of the book it is written of Me) to do Your will, O God." After saying above, "Sacrifices and offerings and whole burnt offerings and sacrifices for sin You have not desired, nor have You taken pleasure in them" (which are offered according to the Law), then He said, "Behold, I have come to do Your will." He takes away the first in order to establish the second. By this will we have been sanctified through the offering of the body of Jesus Christ once for all.

Every priest stands daily ministering and offering time after time the same sacrifices, which can never take away sins; but He, having offered one sacrifice for sins for all time, sat down at the right hand of God, waiting from that time onward until His enemies be made a footstool for His feet. For by one offering He has perfected for all time those who are sanctified.

OUR FATHER, You have displayed
    Your wisdom, Your eternal power,
    Your deity, and Your goodness in nature.[1]
All creation proclaims Your glory,
    and the heavens declare the works of Your hands.
There is no speech or words; no actual voice is heard,
    but the message has gone out throughout all the world.[2]
The proof of Your existence is there in abundance for all to see.
Only an utter fool would ever say in his heart,
    "There is no God."[3]

Still, the truth of the gospel is disclosed to us explicitly
    only by special revelation in the written Word.
The Scriptures are no human invention,
    but under the sovereign guidance of Your Spirit
    the very words You chose were penned[4]
        and have been preserved, translated, published, and multiplied
            so that through the ages the promise of
                forgiveness and eternal life
            has likewise gone out throughout all the world.

In nature we see evidence of
    Your infinite wisdom,
    Your vast, eternal power,
    Your love of beauty,
    Your wonderful greatness,
    and Your sovereign command
        of all that You have made.

But it is only through the gospel
    that we begin to understand the wonder of Your grace,

---

1. Romans 1:19-20
2. Psalm 1:1-4
3. Psalm 14:1
4. 2 Peter 1:21

Your tenderhearted love for sinners like us,
　and the mysteries of divine wisdom that decreed
　　the entire plan of salvation long ages ago, in eternity past.[1]
In accord with that perfect design and sovereign decree,
　　You now grant full and free pardon to sinners
　　　　while upholding the inflexible demands
　　　　　　of perfect righteousness.
You justify sinners in a way that perfectly vindicates
　　the spotless perfection of Your own holiness.[2]
You accomplished this through the sacrifice of Christ,
　　the spotless lamb of God, who paid the price of sin in full.[3]

Thank You, Lord, for drawing us to Yourself.
You opened our blind eyes to see our desperate need for salvation.
You moved our stubborn wills to repent of our sin.
You awakened our cold, dead hearts to believe in Christ.
As we come now to worship You in prayer, we approach with
　　　　profound gratitude,
　　　　heartfelt contrition,
　　　　and deep humility.
Yet we come with the holy boldness of those who know by faith
　　that You pardon iniquity and graciously pass over
　　　　our rebellious acts.
You do not retain your anger forever,
　　because You delight in unchanging love.[4]
You, Lord, are good, and ready to forgive,
　　and abundant in lovingkindness to all who call upon You.[5]

So we come to worship You as those who have been saved,

---

1. Titus 1:2
2. Romans 3:26
3. John 1:29
4. Micah 7:18
5. Psalm 86:5

ever mindful and forever grateful that Christ our Savior
    has rescued us from sin, Satan, death, and hell.
You have chosen to magnify Your name in us.
You have chosen to favor us.
You have poured out Your mercy and grace upon us.

There are no words adequate to express our praise and gratitude,
    and we are too weak and sinful to honor You as we should.
Therefore we long to be glorified,
    so that in the bliss of a heavenly eternity,
    we will finally be able to praise You
        with true and unceasing praise,
        in a manner that befits Your glory.

Meanwhile, we thank You for patiently loving us with an
    undying, unstinting, unbreakable, and inseparable love.
We long to love You as You love us.
But knowing the feeble infirmities of our own fallen hearts,
    we can only look by faith to the once-for-all forgiveness
        purchased for us at the cross of Christ,
        and pledge our eternal love to Christ by faith.
Seal that commitment by Your Spirit
    even as we worship You now in Your Son's name. Amen.

CONTEMPLATING THE CROSS AND FINDING CONTENTMENT

GALATIANS 3:1-14

Y*ou foolish Galatians, who has bewitched you, before whose eyes Jesus Christ was publicly portrayed as crucified? This is the only thing I want to find out from you: did you receive the Spirit by the works of the Law, or by hearing with faith? Are you so foolish? Having begun by the Spirit, are you now being perfected by the flesh? Did you suffer so many things in vain—if indeed it was in vain? So then, does He who provides you with the Spirit and works miracles among you, do it by the works of the Law, or by hearing with faith?*

Even so Abraham believed God, and it was reckoned to him as righteousness. Therefore, be sure that it is those who are of faith who are sons of Abraham. The Scripture, foreseeing that God would justify the Gentiles by faith, preached the gospel beforehand to Abraham, saying, "All the nations will be blessed in you." So then those who are of faith are blessed with Abraham, the believer.

For as many as are of the works of the Law are under a curse; for it is written, "Cursed is everyone who does not abide by all things written in the book of the Law, to perform them." Now that no one is justified by the Law before God is evident; for, "The righteous man shall live by faith." However, the Law is not of faith; on the contrary, "He who practices them shall live by them." Christ redeemed us from the curse of the Law, having become a curse for us—for it is written, "Cursed is everyone who hangs on a tree"—in order

*that in Christ Jesus the blessing of Abraham might come to the Gentiles, so
that we would receive the promise of the Spirit through faith.*

GRACIOUS FATHER, our pride is utterly extinguished
    by the sheer perfection of Your law.
We confess that the law is holy, just, and good.[1]
It is an expression of Your own divine perfection.
It reveals to us in an unmistakable way
    what authentic righteousness requires of us.
Its moral standard is authoritative.
Its principles are distilled goodness.
Its precepts show us how to walk uprightly.
Its prohibitions are perfectly just.
The law is honorable in every way.

And yet we must confess that we have sinned,
    and sinned repeatedly,
        against the holy standard of Your law.
We humbly acknowledge that the law condemns us.
It cuts us off without any remedy.
When the law is finished speaking,
    it leaves us with no hope of redemption—
    only the fear of judgment.

That is why we are inexpressibly thankful
    for the good news of the gospel.
The gospel announces that through Christ,
    You have done for us what the law could never do:
        You judged our sin and forever put it away
           without condemning us.[2]

1. Romans 7:12
2. Romans 8:3

Christ has thus opened the way of life
    (even for the very worst of sinners)
    by furnishing us with full and free justification—
    not through any works of our own;
    not by putting us back under slavish obedience to the law;
    but by Christ's sacrifice on the cross,
        together with His already complete,
        already perfect obedience to the law.

He stood in our place as a perfect Substitute,
    not only fulfilling every jot and tittle
        of what the law demands of us,
        but also paying—in full—the due penalty of our sins.
By faith we are united with Him
    and thus we have been made full beneficiaries
        of His spotless perfection.
His death has fully reconciled us to You;
    and His life supplies all that we need
        to complete our salvation
    by elevating us to a position of unimaginable privilege.[1]

The law had left us destitute and desperate.
One of the most staggering lessons we learn from the law
    is the impossibility of earning salvation for ourselves
        by moral acts or religious rites.
Instead, the law compels us to confess
    that sin has brought us to ruin.
By our own wickedness we forfeited Your favor.
We brought on our own heads the law's righteous curse.
We can only acknowledge our guilt with sorrow;
    we cannot remove it or atone for it.

But then the gospel wonderfully answered our dilemma,

---

1. Romans 5:10

supplying in Christ all that we have ever lacked or longed for.
Christ saves us, although we bring to the table
    no merit, no worthiness, no achievement—
    no goodness of our own.
How could we ever adequately express our gratitude for so great salvation?
The good news of everlasting redemption is so wonderful
    that even angels long to understand it better.[1]

Now when we ponder the cross,
    we are reminded of how much Christ has done for us.
There we also learn the need to separate ourselves from worldly vanities.
There we see the extent of true humility.
There we find assurance of our salvation,
    motivation for self-denial,
    hope to cheer our troubled hearts,
    love to energize our obedience,
    a grand example to guide our footsteps,
    and a powerful reminder that our only reasonable service
        is to become living sacrifices of praise.[2]

So we stand now in prayer under the shadow of the cross,
    realizing that this is the only place
    we could ever find true contentment
        amid the difficulties of life's trials and heartaches.
Here is where all our needs are met—and more.

We can only plead, dear Lord,
    that even though we are fully committed by faith
        to these high and lofty truths,
    we are still sinners in need
        of Your daily forgiveness and mercy.

1. 1 Peter 1:8-12
2. Romans 12:1-2

We have begun our walk of faith in the Spirit
    and we know that we will never be perfected
        through the energies of our own flesh.
O Spirit of God, make us like Christ, in whose name we pray,
    for we depend on You! Amen.

REALIZING THE GREAT COST OF SALVATION

GALATIANS 4:21–5:1

Tell me, you who want to be under law, do you not listen to the law? For it is written that Abraham had two sons, one by the bondwoman and one by the free woman. But the son by the bondwoman was born according to the flesh, and the son by the free woman through the promise. This is allegorically speaking, for these women are two covenants: one proceeding from Mount Sinai bearing children who are to be slaves; she is Hagar. Now this Hagar is Mount Sinai in Arabia and corresponds to the present Jerusalem, for she is in slavery with her children. But the Jerusalem above is free; she is our mother. For it is written, "Rejoice, barren woman who does not bear; break forth and shout, you who are not in labor; for more numerous are the children of the desolate than of the one who has a husband."

And you brethren, like Isaac, are children of promise. But as at that time he who was born according to the flesh persecuted him who was born according to the Spirit, so it is now also. But what does the Scripture say? "Cast out the bondwoman and her son, for the son of the bondwoman shall not be an heir with the son of the free woman." So then, brethren, we are not children of a bondwoman, but of the free woman.

It was for freedom that Christ set us free; therefore keep standing firm and do not be subject again to a yoke of slavery.

OUR LOVING HEAVENLY FATHER,

You graciously gave Your Son as a sacrifice for our sins.
He obediently took our sins to the cross,
   where He bore unspeakable judgment on our behalf
      in accordance with Your perfect will.
You powerfully declared Him to be the true Son of God
   by raising Him from the dead.[1]
And now through Your precious Spirit
   You earnestly invite all who hunger and all who thirst
   to come (penitently yet boldly) and partake freely
      of the bread of heaven and the water of life—
      without money, and without price.[2]

Those blessings are given freely to us;
   but they were not obtained for us without cost to You.
They cost You Your only begotten Son, and they cost Him His life.
He bore the curse incurred by our sin.
When the law thundered against us like Mount Sinai—
   threatening us with condemnation,
   pronouncing our doom,
   and consigning us to the darkness of hell[3]—
      Christ silenced the law's claim against us
         by taking the condemnation upon Himself.
He paid, once for all, the awful price.
We could never have fully discharged that debt to Your justice,
   even if we suffered an eternity of torment in hell.

So we owe Him everything we are.
We were deeply stained,
   guilty of countless sins (both careless and deliberate).
Our sins had cut us off from heaven,

---

1. Romans 1:4
2. Isaiah 55:1-7
3. Hebrews 12:18-29

excluded us from the commonwealth of Israel,
    left us total strangers to the covenants of promise—
        without hope and without God in the world.[1]
But then the blessed good news came to us.
The gospel declared to us the way of life.
Truly it is the power of God for salvation
    to everyone who believes.[2]
Your Spirit graciously drew us into the household of faith
    and You adopted us into the family
        of Your redeemed children.

The human mind simply cannot fathom
    the magnitude of our debt to Your grace.
Nor is the human tongue capable of adequately expressing
    the fullness of our gratitude for so many undeserved mercies.

We know that there is no merit and no atoning value
    in our good works, our prayers,
        our tears, or our good intentions.
Only the atoning blood of Christ
    could ever make an appropriate satisfaction for our sins
        before You.[3]
Therefore we were not redeemed with perishable things
    like silver or gold,
        but with that precious blood,
            shed by the spotless lamb of God.
This was the plan of salvation You ordained
    before the foundation of the world, for our sake.[4]

When we ponder these truths carefully,
    we are astonished that You would save rebellious sinners.

---

1. Ephesians 2:12
2. Romans 1:16
3. Hebrews 9:22-28
4. 1 Peter 1:18-21

Why should guilty evildoers like us
    be washed in the atoning blood of Your Son
        and clothed in His righteousness?
Why should we be allowed
    to radiate the bright glory that belongs only to You?
Why should we be advanced to such a high and eternal state?
Why would You choose us to adoption as Your children,
    even before the foundation of the world?
Such knowledge is too wonderful for us;
    it is high; we cannot attain it.[1]

But we can thank You for Your kindness.
We can only do so in a feeble and inadequate way.
But in the name of Christ our Savior
    we offer what we can of our heartfelt gratitude.
Please receive our worship, loosen our tongues,
        sanctify our lips, and enlarge our hearts
    to worship you more fittingly than we are currently able.
And may our service be acceptable in Your sight. Amen.

---

1. Psalm 139:6

WEEK 29

DESIRING TO BE
MORE THANKFUL

Ephesians 2:1-10

You were dead in your trespasses and sins, in which you formerly walked according to the course of this world, according to the prince of the power of the air, of the spirit that is now working in the sons of disobedience. Among them we too all formerly lived in the lusts of our flesh, indulging the desires of the flesh and of the mind, and were by nature children of wrath, even as the rest. But God, being rich in mercy, because of His great love with which He loved us, even when we were dead in our transgressions, made us alive together with Christ (by grace you have been saved), and raised us up with Him, and seated us with Him in the heavenly places in Christ Jesus, so that in the ages to come He might show the surpassing riches of His grace in kindness toward us in Christ Jesus. For by grace you have been saved through faith; and that not of yourselves, it is the gift of God; not as a result of works, so that no one may boast. For we are His workmanship, created in Christ Jesus for good works, which God prepared beforehand so that we would walk in them.

Glorious Father in heaven,

we again recognize the humbling reality of the gospel,
that salvation is a gift You give by grace through faith alone.

No work of ours, no ritual we perform, no effort we expend
    could ever add an ounce of merit to the finished work of Christ.

In our fallen state we were living under Your wrath,
    driven by sinful passions,
    seeking only the gratification of our flesh,
    unable to convert ourselves—
    unable even to prepare our hearts
        for Your saving work.
We were spiritually dead.
Our wills were in bondage to sin,
    so that we were spiritually insensible and wholly incapable
        of doing anything to please You.
Even now, we can do no good toward our own salvation.
The only good deeds we do are works
    You sovereignly and graciously prepared for us
        before we ever thought to do them.
And it is You alone who empowers us to walk
    in accord with Your holy plan.

What a blow that truth is to our religious and moral achievements!

Yet we affirm the testimony of the great apostle Paul regarding
        religious ceremony, ethnic heritage,
        legal observances, personal achievement,
        human zeal, and every other excuse
    for mortal boasting.
All such traits are no assets at all in Your sight,
    and we count them as pure rubbish.[1]
We also echo Paul's personal confession:
    "I know that nothing good dwells in me, that is, in my flesh."[2]
Like Him, we count even the best attainments of our fleshly efforts as loss
    in view of the surpassing value of knowing Christ Jesus as Lord.

1. Philippians 3:8
2. Romans 7:18

All we seek now is to be found in Him,
>not having a righteousness of our own derived from the law,
>but that which is through faith in Christ alone.[1]

Father of glory, fill us with gratitude
>that befits the grace You have shown us.
Open our hearts and fill them with praise for You.
Remove every vestige of fleshly pride from our hearts
>as we contemplate the surpassing greatness of Christ
>>and His righteousness.

On the one hand, we come before You
>rejoicing that we have been saved by Your grace.
But on the other we come as
>broken, penitent, humble sinners,
>remembering that we are altogether unworthy of Your favor.
We thank You for granting us the repentance that leads to life[2]
>and for reconciling us to Yourself
>>through faith in Jesus Christ.
By faith alone we have been brought to the place
>where all our sins are forgiven
>>and we rest secure in the hope of heaven.

We desire, Lord, that our prayers and lives
>would overflow with worship,
>motivated by sincere love for You.
Thank You for enabling us by Your Holy Spirit,
>who not only radiates divine love into our hearts,[3]
>but also purifies, strengthens, and encourages us
>>so we might serve You in a way
>>that adorns Your greatness.

---

1. Philippians 3:9
2. Acts 11:18
3. Romans 5:5

Hear our prayer as we ask for all the fullness
      of Your spiritual provision—
      so that we might be all You want us to be—
      in the name of Christ. Amen.

REMEMBERING WHAT WE WERE RESCUED FROM

2 Corinthians 5

We know that if the earthly tent which is our house is torn down, we have a building from God, a house not made with hands, eternal in the heavens. For indeed in this house we groan, longing to be clothed with our dwelling from heaven, inasmuch as we, having put it on, will not be found naked. For indeed while we are in this tent, we groan, being burdened, because we do not want to be unclothed but to be clothed, so that what is mortal will be swallowed up by life. Now He who prepared us for this very purpose is God, who gave to us the Spirit as a pledge.

Therefore, being always of good courage, and knowing that while we are at home in the body we are absent from the Lord—for we walk by faith, not by sight—we are of good courage, I say, and prefer rather to be absent from the body and to be at home with the Lord. Therefore we also have as our ambition, whether at home or absent, to be pleasing to Him. For we must all appear before the judgment seat of Christ, so that each one may be recompensed for his deeds in the body, according to what he has done, whether good or bad.

Therefore, knowing the fear of the Lord, we persuade men, but we are made manifest to God; and I hope that we are made manifest also in your consciences. We are not again commending ourselves to you but are giving you an occasion to be proud of us, so that you will have an answer for those who take pride in appearance and not in heart. For if we are beside ourselves, it is for God; if we are of sound mind, it is for you. For the love of Christ controls us, having concluded this, that one died for all, therefore all died; and

He died for all, so that they who live might no longer live for themselves, but for Him who died and rose again on their behalf.

Therefore from now on we recognize no one according to the flesh; even though we have known Christ according to the flesh, yet now we know Him in this way no longer. Therefore if anyone is in Christ, he is a new creature; the old things passed away; behold, new things have come. Now all these things are from God, who reconciled us to Himself through Christ and gave us the ministry of reconciliation, namely, that God was in Christ reconciling the world to Himself, not counting their trespasses against them, and He has committed to us the word of reconciliation.

Therefore, we are ambassadors for Christ, as though God were making an appeal through us; we beg you on behalf of Christ, be reconciled to God. He made Him who knew no sin to be sin on our behalf, so that we might become the righteousness of God in Him.

FATHER, through the cross of Christ
we have been reconciled to You,
and we exult in the hope of future glory.[1]
In the meantime, we plead for grace
to walk uprightly each day of our lives
under the power of Your sanctifying hand.
We are instructed by Your Word to thank You even for our troubles,
because we know You use them to work Your character in us.
Give us clarity of mind and purity of heart to embrace that truth,
that we might enthusiastically rejoice in our trials,
knowing that suffering produces Christlike character.[2]

How grateful we are that through the death of Christ
we have been saved from Your wrath,

1. Romans 5:2
2. Romans 5:3

forgiven our transgressions,
washed from all guilt,
freed from the law's condemnation,
and declared righteous before the very throne of heaven!
You not only reconciled us to Yourself through Christ;
You also commissioned us to be ministers of reconciliation.
May we be faithful and fearless ambassadors,
proclaiming the good news
and beseeching sinners to be reconciled.

Keep us humble, Father.
May we always be mindful of what we are in ourselves.
We are fallen creatures,
without merit of our own,
guilty to the core of our beings,
justly deserving everlasting destruction.
You initiated the reconciliation;
You sent us a Savior, who is Christ the Lord;[1]
He supplied everything we need
by way of righteousness and redemption.
We have nothing of which to boast,[2]
and everything to be thankful for.[3]

You are the One who opened our understanding to see the gospel,
and then You opened our hearts to embrace it.[4]
Your Spirit revealed to us the hidden wisdom
which even the rulers of this age do not understand.[5]
You gave Your Son to die in our place, and with Him,
You freely gave us everything we lack.[6]

---

1. Luke 2:10-11
2. Ephesians 2:9
3. 1 Thessalonians 5:18
4. Acts 16:14
5. 1 Corinthians 2:7-8
6. Romans 8:32

Nothing we could ever do can augment or add merit
    to what You have already accomplished on our behalf.
We simply rest in the perfect, finished work of Christ.

We receive Your love with glad and humble hearts, dear Father.
May the Spirit of wisdom and revelation unfold to us
    a yet more intimate knowledge of You.
May the eyes of our hearts be enlightened.
May we know what is the hope of Your calling.
May we realize the riches of the glory of Your inheritance.
And may we experience the surpassing greatness of Your power.[1]

We thank You that the work of Christ
    is applied to us effectually and continually.
We know that we are thereby secure
    in the forgiveness Christ won for us at Calvary.
Strengthen our faith,
    seal our wills unto obedience,
    and empower our lives to glorify You.

In the blessed name of Christ we pray. Amen.

---

1. Ephesians 1:11-19

BEING IN AWE OVER OUR NARROW ESCAPE

MATTHEW 7:13-27

Enter through the narrow gate; for the gate is wide and the way is broad that leads to destruction, and there are many who enter through it. For the gate is small and the way is narrow that leads to life, and there are few who find it.

Beware of the false prophets, who come to you in sheep's clothing, but inwardly are ravenous wolves. You will know them by their fruits. Grapes are not gathered from thorn bushes nor figs from thistles, are they? So every good tree bears good fruit, but the bad tree bears bad fruit. A good tree cannot produce bad fruit, nor can a bad tree produce good fruit. Every tree that does not bear good fruit is cut down and thrown into the fire. So then, you will know them by their fruits.

Not everyone who says to Me, "Lord, Lord," will enter the kingdom of heaven, but he who does the will of My Father who is in heaven will enter. Many will say to Me on that day, "Lord, Lord, did we not prophesy in Your name, and in Your name cast out demons, and in Your name perform many miracles?" And then I will declare to them, "I never knew you; depart from Me, you who practice lawlessness."

Therefore everyone who hears these words of Mine and acts on them, may be compared to a wise man who built his house on the rock. And the rain fell, and the floods came, and the winds blew and slammed against that house; and yet it did not fall, for it had been founded on the rock. Everyone who hears these words of Mine and does not act on them, will be like a foolish man who

built his house on the sand. The rain fell, and the floods came, and the winds
blew and slammed against that house; and it fell—and great was its fall.

EVERLASTING GOD and Father of our Lord Jesus Christ,
   we think of the narrow and broad ways Jesus spoke about.
We realize that vast numbers of humanity
    are blithely headed for eternal judgment,
   and we confess that we ourselves
      are in every way worthy of such judgment.

By nature we are corrupt and defiled.
Our wills are in bondage to our own fleshly desires.
Our very souls are ruined, lifeless, and utterly profane
    because of our sin.
By ourselves we are without strength,
    without merit, without hope,
     and unable to lift ourselves up from that fallen condition.

But we have found our hope in Christ,
    who opened the narrow way
      and ushered us through the small gate.
We are grateful recipients of Your abundant mercy
    and the exceeding riches of Your grace,
    all made available freely to us from the hand of Christ.
In Him we have redemption through His blood,
    the forgiveness of sins, according to the riches of His grace,
    which He lavished on us unsparingly.[1]

Thank You, Lord, for loving us enough
    to rescue us from sin, death, and hell.

---

1. Ephesians 1:7-8

Although by rights we should have been destroyed,[1]
    You freely granted us forgiveness, life, and the bliss of heaven.
You sent us the perfect Mediator,
        our blessed Redeemer,
        the man Christ Jesus.[2]
For the joy set before Him, He endured the cross, despising the shame,[3]
        discounting the horror of bearing the great weight of all our sins,
            and bearing our judgment in His own body—
            so that we might die to sin and live unto holiness.[4]

How horrible that must have been for the eternally Holy One
        who prayed, "Father, glorify Me together with Yourself,
        with the glory which I had with You before the world was"![5]
Nevertheless, our Lord Jesus was neither dissuaded nor dispirited,
        but accomplished the work You gave Him to do,
        declaring triumphantly with His dying breath,
            "It is finished!"[6]

Christ thus suffered for our iniquities;
        He bore our sorrows;
        He paid our penalty;
        He removed our guilt;
        He bought our redemption;
        He fulfilled all righteousness;
        He justified multitudes;
        He brought glory to Your Name;
        and He fulfilled all Your good pleasure.[7]
By His work justice was fully satisfied,

---

1. Malachi 3:6
2. 1 Timothy 2:5
3. Hebrews 12:2
4. 1 Peter 2:24
5. John 17:5; Hebrews 12:2
6. John 19:30; John 17:4
7. Isaiah 53:4-11

Christ Himself was vindicated,
Your law was upheld,
the truth of the gospel was established,
and Your eternal love was powerfully put on display.
Enlarge our poor hearts to apprehend these truths better,
and fill our mouths with humble thanks.

Lord, we need ongoing cleansing so we may come before You
with clean hands and a pure heart.[1]
We enter into Your presence on our knees with joy,
anticipating Your peace and blessing.
Filled with hope, we look forward
to that glorious eternity awaiting us in heaven,
where we will worship You perfectly.
Until then we bow before You with imperfect adoration,
but with our feeble powers strengthened by Your Spirit,
we offer You praise in the name of the Lord Jesus. Amen.

---

1. Psalm 24:3-4

PRAYERS
ON PERSONAL
HOLINESS

LONGING FOR CONTINUAL CLEANSING

1 JOHN 1

W*hat was from the beginning, what we have heard, what we have seen with our eyes, what we have looked at and touched with our hands, concerning the Word of Life—and the life was manifested, and we have seen and testify and proclaim to you the eternal life, which was with the Father and was manifested to us—what we have seen and heard we proclaim to you also, so that you too may have fellowship with us; and indeed our fellowship is with the Father, and with His Son Jesus Christ. These things we write, so that our joy may be made complete.*

This is the message we have heard from Him and announce to you, that God is Light, and in Him there is no darkness at all. If we say that we have fellowship with Him and yet walk in the darkness, we lie and do not practice the truth; but if we walk in the Light as He Himself is in the Light, we have fellowship with one another, and the blood of Jesus His Son cleanses us from all sin. If we say that we have no sin, we are deceiving ourselves and the truth is not in us. If we confess our sins, He is faithful and righteous to forgive us our sins and to cleanse us from all unrighteousness. If we say that we have not sinned, we make Him a liar and His word is not in us.

WE COME BEFORE YOU, our great God and eternal King,

acknowledging that we are sinful,
  not only in that we *have* sinned, but also that we *do* sin.
We want no self-deception about that:
  Your Word makes it clear if we denied our sin,
  we would be calling You a liar!
Our sin is ever before us, to echo King David's prayer,[1]
  so we want first to confess our sins,
    knowing You are faithful to forgive us
      and that You bring Your righteousness to bear
        in cleansing us of each day's sinful accumulations.

In the same breath we also thank You, heavenly Father,
  for the glories of the gospel of our Lord Jesus Christ,
  especially the fellowship we enjoy together
    with You and Your Son.
Our tongues cannot find sufficient praise wherewith to bless You.
What You have done for us exceeds all human accolades.
Our poor minds can't begin to fathom the immensity of Your grace,
  but we know that You are far more worthy
    than human language could ever express.
That cannot stop us from trying—
  and we trust that You will receive
    the simple thanks of Your children.

Thank You for the daily mercies You shower us with:
      the comforts and blessings of life,
      the joy of family and friends,
      the love of the church,
      and countless other good things
    that you give us richly to enjoy.[2]
We thank You especially for the Holy Scriptures, the Word of Life,[3]

---

1. Psalm 51:2-4
2. 1 Timothy 6:17
3. Philippians 2:14-16; Acts 5:19-20

for how would we live without Your truth?
It leads us to repentance when we sin,
  it gives us promises to live by,
  and it encourages our hearts
    to love and pursue holiness.
We long for heaven, where we will finally be perfect,
  but for now we live in a world
    where we are still beset by sin, failure, and weakness—
    and we confess that we often stumble and fall.
We desperately need Your constant forgiveness and sustaining grace.
Give us a deeper hunger for righteousness.

We therefore ask, O God, that Your Word
    would dominate our thinking,
    cleanse our consciences,
    and control our living
  so that the glories of Christ and the transforming power of the gospel
    would clearly be on display in us.

Thank You for that continual cleansing from all our sin.
Thank You for the grace that is in Christ Jesus, our Savior.
Thank you for the great love
  with which You drew us to Yourself.
Such divine favor is something we could never earn;
  You have given it simply because we asked in faith
    that You Yourself graciously supplied.[1]
We cling to Christ, in whose name we pray,
  asking in conclusion that through Him
    we might bring honor to Your worthy name. Amen.

---

1. Ephesians 2:8-10

DESIRING STEADY PROGRESS FOR GOOD

1 John 3:1-12

S*ee how great a love the Father has bestowed on us, that we would be called children of God; and such we are. For this reason the world does not know us, because it did not know Him. Beloved, now we are children of God, and it has not appeared as yet what we will be. We know that when He appears, we will be like Him, because we will see Him just as He is. And everyone who has this hope fixed on Him purifies himself, just as He is pure.*

Everyone who practices sin also practices lawlessness; and sin is lawlessness. You know that He appeared in order to take away sins; and in Him there is no sin. No one who abides in Him sins; no one who sins has seen Him or knows Him. Little children, make sure no one deceives you; the one who practices righteousness is righteous, just as He is righteous; the one who practices sin is of the devil; for the devil has sinned from the beginning. The Son of God appeared for this purpose, to destroy the works of the devil. No one who is born of God practices sin, because His seed abides in him; and he cannot sin, because he is born of God. By this the children of God and the children of the devil are obvious: anyone who does not practice righteousness is not of God, nor the one who does not love his brother.

For this is the message which you have heard from the beginning, that we should love one another; not as Cain, who was of the evil one and slew his brother. And for what reason did he slay him? Because his deeds were evil, and his brother's were righteous.

※

FATHER, thank You for the vital truth
    that Your Spirit transforms us.
We know that the transformed life is a fruit,
    not the cause, of our salvation.
You are the One who chose and drew us,
    and Christ is both the Author and Finisher of our faith.
His work is the sole ground and reason for our justification.
We're not saved because of any merit or goodness of our own,
    for we have none.

But we likewise know that when You give us a standing by faith in Christ,
    You completely transform us.
If anyone is in Christ, he is a new creature;
    the old things passed away; behold, new things have come.[1]
Your Spirit gives us new hearts.[2]
From the moment of our conversion, He indwells us,
    and through His living presence in our hearts
        You are steadily conforming us to the image of Christ.[3]

We understand, of course,
    that we will never attain sinless perfection in this life,
    because we won't fully be like Christ
        until we finally see Him face-to-face.[4]
But when we sin, we know that we have an Advocate with the Father,
    Jesus Christ the righteous.[5]
We thank You that He is pleading for us even now,
    seeking our welfare before Your throne
        with prayers that put our paltry prayers to shame.

---

1. 2 Corinthians 5:17
2. Ezekiel 11:19
3. Romans 8:29
4. 1 John 3:19
5. 1 John 2:1

Your Spirit likewise intercedes for us,
> with groanings that cannot be uttered.[1]

More and more, Lord, we are conscious of our guilt
> and ashamed of our sin.
Help us therefore to bless You more and more
> for Your steadfast love toward us.
Empower us more and more
> to serve You with faithfulness and joy.
Above all, make us more and more like Christ.

And remind us, Lord, that we are now slaves of righteousness
> rather than slaves of sin.
We come before You humbly,
> grateful for Your mercy and thankful for the transformation
>> that has caused us to love and do the things that please You.

O God, our Creator and Lord,
> we delight in Your righteousness and wisdom.
We have been blessed by Your mercy and grace.
We rejoice in Your lovingkindness and compassion
> toward sinners like us.
Though we are totally unworthy of Your favor,
> You graciously saved us from the guilt and condemnation
>> of our own sin.
Our judgment was rendered on Christ at Calvary,
> who put away our sins by the sacrifice of Himself,
> and You raised Him from the dead
>> as affirmation of His great accomplishment.

Your mercy and grace were thus secured for us
> by Christ our Savior.
That is why we desire to honor Him through our service.

---

1. Romans 8:26

But may we never think of our own works as meritorious—
    or even as worthy supplements to His finished work.
We confess that our best service
    is altogether unprofitable,
    and when we have rendered our best obedience,
    we are still merely unworthy slaves
        who have done no more than that which we ought to do.[1]

May we therefore forever rely only on Christ,
    trust in Him,
    honor Him,
    and serve Him faithfully but humbly.
We repudiate our sins and trust in Your ongoing cleansing and forgiveness.
Enable us to live in a way
    that draws others to the glories of Christ,
    in whose name we pray. Amen.

---

1. Luke 17:10

EXPERIENCING ALL THAT GOD WOULD HAVE FOR US

1 John 3:13-24

Do not be surprised, brethren, if the world hates you. We know that we have passed out of death into life, because we love the brethren. He who does not love abides in death. Everyone who hates his brother is a murderer; and you know that no murderer has eternal life abiding in him. We know love by this, that He laid down His life for us; and we ought to lay down our lives for the brethren. But whoever has the world's goods, and sees his brother in need and closes his heart against him, how does the love of God abide in him? Little children, let us not love with word or with tongue, but in deed and truth. We will know by this that we are of the truth, and will assure our heart before Him in whatever our heart condemns us; for God is greater than our heart and knows all things. Beloved, if our heart does not condemn us, we have confidence before God; and whatever we ask we receive from Him, because we keep His commandments and do the things that are pleasing in His sight.

This is His commandment, that we believe in the name of His Son Jesus Christ, and love one another, just as He commanded us. The one who keeps His commandments abides in Him, and He in him. We know by this that He abides in us, by the Spirit whom He has given us.

IT IS A WONDER, our God, that You have asked us
    to proclaim the glorious gospel of Jesus Christ to the world,
    knowing that the world hates us.
Because we have passed out of death into life,
        because we love the brethren,
        and because we belong to You,
        the world hates us
    and yet it is the very world we are to reach.
We know then that if we are to reach them,
    it is Your work and not ours—
    Your transforming power that will do the job—
    so we call upon You as we endeavor faithfully
        to live to the honor of Christ and proclaim His gospel.

Thank You, Father, that You gave the Lord Jesus
    to be our great High Priest.
He has given us confidence to enter the holy place
    by a new and living way
        which He inaugurated for us through the veil.[1]
We stand in utter awe before Christ's glory.
We praise Him for the infinite value of His sacrifice,
    the wonderful example of His humility,
    the tenderness of His grace toward us,
    and the blessed assurance we gain by His ongoing intercession
        before Your throne.

We are profoundly indebted
    for the grace You pour out upon us at all times.
It encourages us not to grow weary in our trials.
It calms our fears.
It removes our guilt.
It unfetters us from shame.
It strengthens us in our infirmities.

---

1. Hebrews 10:19-20

It teaches us to deny ungodliness and worldly desires
>   and to live sensibly, righteously, and godly in the present age,
>   looking for the blessed hope and the appearing
>   of the glory of our great God and Savior,
>   Christ Jesus, who gave Himself for us
>   to redeem us from every lawless deed,
>   and to purify for Himself a people
>   for His own possession,
>   zealous for good deeds.[1]

Thank You that this grace
>   restores, leads, guards,
>   supplies, and strengthens us.
It also encourages our hope in a world of difficulty.
Although once poor we are now rich,
>   once bound we are now free,
>   once defeated we are now triumphant.
Our duties call for more grace than we possess,
>   but not more than is found in You.
We know that in Christ we "have been made complete"
>   and that "in Him all the fullness of Deity dwells in bodily form."[2]
How grateful we are that in Him You give us grace upon grace,
>   cover every sin, and forgive every iniquity!

Help us, dear Lord, to experience all You would have for us—
>   whether prosperity or adversity,
>   loss or gain,
>   darkness or light,
>   sickness or health,
>   blessing or suffering.
May we follow joyfully wherever Christ leads us,
>   knowing Your providence is at work in it all,

1. Titus 2:12-14
2. Colossians 2:9-10

Your purposes will be fulfilled,
   and Your grace is always sufficient.
In that confidence we come before Your throne
      to offer these petitions in the exalted name of Christ. Amen.

WEEK 35

AVOIDING HYPOCRISY
AND CRAVING SINCERITY

GALATIANS 5:1-14

I t was for freedom that Christ set us free; therefore keep standing firm and do not be subject again to a yoke of slavery.

Behold I, Paul, say to you that if you receive circumcision, Christ will be of no benefit to you. And I testify again to every man who receives circumcision, that he is under obligation to keep the whole Law. You have been severed from Christ, you who are seeking to be justified by law; you have fallen from grace. For we through the Spirit, by faith, are waiting for the hope of righteousness. For in Christ Jesus neither circumcision nor uncircumcision means anything, but faith working through love.

You were running well; who hindered you from obeying the truth? This persuasion did not come from Him who calls you. A little leaven leavens the whole lump of dough. I have confidence in you in the Lord that you will adopt no other view; but the one who is disturbing you will bear his judgment, whoever he is. But I, brethren, if I still preach circumcision, why am I still persecuted? Then the stumbling block of the cross has been abolished. I wish that those who are troubling you would even mutilate themselves.

For you were called to freedom, brethren; only do not turn your freedom into an opportunity for the flesh, but through love serve one another. For the whole Law is fulfilled in one word, in the statement, "You shall love your neighbor as yourself."

DEAR FATHER, we know that salvation
    does not come through the law.
Much less could any physical rite or ceremonial surgery
    ever save a sinner from the righteous condemnation
        of your judgment.
If the law held forth any hope of salvation
    we would still be bound to keep it in every detail,
    and we know that only the sinless Son of God
        could ever accomplish such perfect obedience.
So salvation by law is an absolute impossibility
    for sinful people like us.

But Christ is the ideal and the fulfillment
    of everything the law ever aimed for[1]—
    including the righteousness You require of us.
Christ fully attained the perfection that is impossible for us.
His righteousness is therefore a perfect covering
    and we lay hold of it by faith in Him.
His sacrifice on our behalf at Calvary
    totally liberates us from the law's condemnation.
His death counts as full punishment for our sins.
His sinless life furnishes the perfect righteousness we lack.
You have thus wholly reconciled us to Yourself through Christ.
He who knew no sin became sin on our behalf,
    so that we might become the righteousness of God in Him.[2]

We acknowledge You as our sovereign Lord.
You hear prayer, and to You all people of faith may freely come.
As for our transgressions, You forgive them.[3]
You answer us in righteousness.
You establish the mountains;

---

1. Romans 10:4

2. 2 Corinthians 5:21

3. Psalm 65:2-3

You still the roaring of the seas;
You suppress the tumult of the peoples.
Those who dwell in the ends of the earth stand in awe.
You make even the dawn and the sunset shout for joy.[1]

How we thank You for prompting our hearts
to believe, receive, and embrace
the truth of Your Word,
the work of Your Son,
the fullness of Your Spirit,
and the blessing of Your salvation.

We confess, righteous Lord, that we are unworthy
of Your favor and forgiveness.
We have sinned—repeatedly—and done what is evil in Your sight.[2]
Our iniquities are more numerous than the hairs of our heads.[3]
Our transgressions are multiplied before You,
and our sins testify against us.
We know our own iniquities all too well.
We have transgressed and denied the Lord.
We have turned away from our God.
We have spoken evil.
And we have conceived evil in our hearts.[4]
Of all those things we are shamefully guilty;
we have no excuse and no plea but Your mercy.
Be merciful to us; pardon our iniquities;
and bless us with abundant grace
that we might live holy lives that honor You.

We desire to serve You from the heart
as a sincere expression of the same righteous love

1. Psalm 65:5-8
2. Psalm 51:4
3. Psalm 40:12
4. Isaiah 59:12

with which You loved us
  and drew us into the fellowship of faith.
Help us to hate hypocrisy more in our own hearts
  than when we suspect it in others.
Clothe us with humility
  and lead us in the paths of righteousness
    for Your name's sake.[1]
Loose our tongues to speak of the glory of Your kingdom
  and talk of Your power.[2]
May our confession of Christ and our testimony about Him to others
  be wholehearted and true.

May we persevere in the faith until we see You face to face.
We look forward eagerly to that day!
In Christ's worthy name we pray. Amen.

---

1. Psalm 23:3
2. Psalm 145:11

LONGING FOR THE FRUIT OF THE SPIRIT

GALATIANS 5:16-26

I say, walk by the Spirit, and you will not carry out the desire of the flesh. For the flesh sets its desire against the Spirit, and the Spirit against the flesh; for these are in opposition to one another, so that you may not do the things that you please. But if you are led by the Spirit, you are not under the Law. Now the deeds of the flesh are evident, which are: immorality, impurity, sensuality, idolatry, sorcery, enmities, strife, jealousy, outbursts of anger, disputes, dissensions, factions, envying, drunkenness, carousing, and things like these, of which I forewarn you, just as I have forewarned you, that those who practice such things will not inherit the kingdom of God. But the fruit of the Spirit is love, joy, peace, patience, kindness, goodness, faithfulness, gentleness, self-control; against such things there is no law. Now those who belong to Christ Jesus have crucified the flesh with its passions and desires.

If we live by the Spirit, let us also walk by the Spirit. Let us not become boastful, challenging one another, envying one another.

OUR FATHER, Your Word makes it clear
   there are only two ways to live:
   by the flesh or by Your Spirit.

One is sinful and the other holy.
One represents those who are without hope and without You;
      the other is characteristic of those who belong to You.
Empower us by Your Spirit to be people
      who are loving, joyful, peaceful, patient, kind, good,
      gentle, faithful, and self-restrained.
Since we live by the Spirit—our spiritual life comes from Him—
      we beg You to help us walk daily in His strength.
Anything less is neither worthy of You
      nor consistent with our new nature as Christians.

You, our God, are the source of all life.
We were by nature dead in trespasses and sins,
      in bondage to the lusts of our flesh,
      indulging the desires of the flesh and of the mind—
      children of wrath.[1]
You alone could redeem us from the curse of our sin.
Even now we stand in desperate need
      of Your mercy and grace, and we are thankful
            that You are slow to anger and great in lovingkindness.[2]

We yield ourselves up to You as living sacrifices.[3]
We rightly belong to You—all of us;
      every aspect of our being—
      body, soul, spirit, intellect, will, and affections.
Grant that we would have purified minds
      to seek and obey divine truth.
Give us cleansed hearts to love You better.
Give us right spirits to serve You more faithfully.
And give us a new disposition that desires Your will rather than our own.

---

1. Ephesians 2:1-3
2. Psalm 145:8
3. Romans 12:1-2

O gracious Father, hear our prayer and empower us to live
    in a way that gives honor
        to the One who has given salvation so freely to us!
Let not our vision of Christ be clouded or blurred
    whether by deliberate sin or by careless negligence.
May we not trifle away our lives
    in foolish or worldly pursuits.
May we instead make the most of every opportunity
    for service, ministry, and worship.
Take us by the hand to keep us from stumbling.

Never allow us to do anything that would cause
    Your truth to be obscured,
    Your people to be injured,
    Your name to be dishonored,
    Your Spirit to be grieved,
    or Your Son to be blasphemed.
May all our labors be useful
    to accomplish Your will on earth as it is in heaven.[1]

Keep us ever mindful of the grace that drew us to Christ,
    the blood that cleanses us,
    the righteousness that justifies us,
    and the truth that sanctifies us.
We long to love You with all our heart, soul, mind, and strength—
    but to do that we need the Spirit.
May He control us completely so that we live for Your glory,
    to the praise of Christ,
    in whose name we pray. Amen.

---

1. Matthew 6:10

WEEK 37

LAMENTING OVER SIN

ROMANS 1:16-32

I am not ashamed of the gospel, for it is the power of God for salvation to everyone who believes, to the Jew first and also to the Greek. For in it the righteousness of God is revealed from faith to faith; as it is written, "But the righteous man shall live by faith."

For the wrath of God is revealed from heaven against all ungodliness and unrighteousness of men who suppress the truth in unrighteousness, because that which is known about God is evident within them; for God made it evident to them. For since the creation of the world His invisible attributes, His eternal power and divine nature, have been clearly seen, being understood through what has been made, so that they are without excuse. For even though they knew God, they did not honor Him as God or give thanks, but they became futile in their speculations, and their foolish heart was darkened. Professing to be wise, they became fools, and exchanged the glory of the incorruptible God for an image in the form of corruptible man and of birds and four-footed animals and crawling creatures.

Therefore God gave them over in the lusts of their hearts to impurity, so that their bodies would be dishonored among them. For they exchanged the truth of God for a lie, and worshiped and served the creature rather than the Creator, who is blessed forever. Amen.

For this reason God gave them over to degrading passions; for their women exchanged the natural function for that which is unnatural, and in the same way also the men abandoned the natural function of the woman and burned in their desire toward one another, men with men committing indecent acts and receiving in their own persons the due penalty of their error.

And just as they did not see fit to acknowledge God any longer, God gave them over to a depraved mind, to do those things which are not proper, being filled with all unrighteousness, wickedness, greed, evil; full of envy, murder, strife, deceit, malice; they are gossips, slanderers, haters of God, insolent, arrogant, boastful, inventors of evil, disobedient to parents, without understanding, untrustworthy, unloving, unmerciful; and although they know the ordinance of God, that those who practice such things are worthy of death, they not only do the same, but also give hearty approval to those who practice them.

O GOD OF GRACE, were it not for Your call upon our lives,
  the vices of the world would utterly destroy us.
Apart from Your love and provision in Christ,
  we would have no hope.
When we were wretched sinners,
    alienated from You,
    undone, full of evil desires,
    in bondage to evil—
  instead of abandoning us to our own iniquities
    and their consequences,
    You reached out to us and drew us to Yourself.
The gospel came in the power of the Holy Spirit
  and rescued us from ruin.
Christ, our great Deliverer, freed us from
  sin, death, and judgment.

You imputed our sin to the Lord Jesus Christ,
  and He bore the full penalty.
He condemned sin in the flesh.[1]

---

1. Romans 8:3

He redeemed us from the curse of the law,
    having become a curse for us.[1]
Now you credit His righteousness to us,
    and we receive divine favor that belongs to Him.
You justify the ungodly.[2]
There is therefore now no condemnation
    for those who are in Christ Jesus.[3]

Even though we have been fully forgiven and entirely reconciled to You,
    sin still clings to us.
We know that in our flesh dwells no good thing.
The willing is present with us, but the doing of good is not.
Sinful desires and evil habits hound and harass us,
    although we want to do good.[4]

We stand like Lazarus:
    We have been given new life at the call of our Savior,
    being raised from the dead,
    but our grave clothes still remain.[5]
We are like the prodigal son,
    returning from the far country filthy, destitute,
    still wearing the rags of our dereliction
        and still bearing the scars of sin.
We long for that day when we leave this world
    and receive eternal, unblemished holiness
        through instant glorification.
Then we will finally be unspotted in Your presence,
    and we will dwell forever
        in perfect righteousness and consummate holiness.

1. Galatians 3:13
2. Romans 4:5
3. Romans 8:1
4. Romans 7:18,21
5. John 11:35-45

Until then, Lord, cleanse us daily.
Intensify our distaste for sin.
Magnify Christ in our eyes.
Amplify Your truth in our hearts.
Mortify sin in our lives.
Crucify our sinful self-love.

We adore You, Lord, and we offer You these prayers
    as an act of worship in our Savior's name. Amen.

BEING MADE CAPABLE
OF PLEASING GOD

ROMANS 2:1-16

Y ou have no excuse, everyone of you who passes judgment, for in that which you judge another, you condemn yourself; for you who judge practice the same things. And we know that the judgment of God rightly falls upon those who practice such things. But do you suppose this, O man, when you pass judgment on those who practice such things and do the same yourself, that you will escape the judgment of God? Or do you think lightly of the riches of His kindness and tolerance and patience, not knowing that the kindness of God leads you to repentance? But because of your stubbornness and unrepentant heart you are storing up wrath for yourself in the day of wrath and revelation of the righteous judgment of God, who will render to each person according to his deeds: to those who by perseverance in doing good seek for glory and honor and immortality, eternal life; but to those who are selfishly ambitious and do not obey the truth, but obey unrighteousness, wrath and indignation. There will be tribulation and distress for every soul of man who does evil, of the Jew first and also of the Greek, but glory and honor and peace to everyone who does good, to the Jew first and also to the Greek. For there is no partiality with God.

For all who have sinned without the Law will also perish without the Law, and all who have sinned under the Law will be judged by the Law; for it is not the hearers of the Law who are just before God, but the doers of the Law will be justified. For when Gentiles who do not have the Law do instinctively the things of the Law, these, not having the Law, are a law to themselves, in that they show the work of the Law written in their hearts, *their conscience bearing witness and their thoughts alternately accusing or else defending them, on the day when, according to my gospel, God will judge the secrets of men through Christ Jesus.*

OUR FATHER, how can we who are born sinners,
    who can do nothing to please You,
      seek—let alone *find*—glory, honor, and immortality?
How can we be delivered from selfish ambition
    and disobedience to the truth?
How can we escape Your just wrath, indignation, and judgment?
We affirm the pure righteousness of Your law,
    which expresses Your holy nature
      as written in Scripture and in the human conscience.
We know what is right and wrong,
    yet more often than not we find ourselves
      in the wrong and unable to do right.[1]

How thankful we are for Christ's work
    and Your Spirit enabling us to put our trust in Jesus as Lord!
In the moment we first believed, You granted us
    a new life, a new heart, and new, holy affections.
Thus regenerated, we now have by Your gracious hand a new capacity
    to do what is good, honorable, and righteous.
We praise You that in Christ
    we have been made capable of pleasing You.
In what better way can we thank You,
    and for what greater end have we been made?
With humility we seek always to remember
    that the will and the power to do right
      come only from You.

1. Romans 2:1-16

Immortal, invisible, all-wise and most glorious God,
    You have sovereignly enabled us to
        know the truth,
        love the truth,
        live the truth,
        proclaim the truth,
        and worship You in spirit and in truth.
Yet as we face the reality of our daily lives,
    we know that sin still exists within us
        and will seek to subdue us
            until we reach heavenly glory.
We mourn over our sin; we hunger and thirst after righteousness;[1]
    we joyfully concur with the law of God in the inner man.[2]
Help us to put off the old things and put on the new—
    and be renewed in the spirit of our minds.[3]

May we faithfully follow the humble example of our Lord.
May we love Him sincerely,
    glory in His cross,
    pursue what is holy,
    and shun all that is shameful and wicked.

Give us courage and boldness, combined with graciousness,
    to confess the Redeemer before lost men and women—
    our neighbors, co-workers, and even our earthly adversaries.
May we willingly bear Christ's reproach;
    may we clearly communicate His love;
    may we thoroughly be controlled by His Spirit;
    and may we faithfully walk in His steps.

Fill us with divine wisdom from Your Word.

---

1. Matthew 5:3-6
2. Romans 7:22
3. Ephesians 4:22-24

Help us, Lord, to live in a way
    that presents Jesus Christ as all-glorious
        and draws sinners to the Holy One.
These things we pray in His name. Amen.

BEING THANKFUL FOR THAT WHICH COVERS ALL INIQUITIES

ROMANS 3:10-20

As it is written, "There is none righteous, not even one; there is none who understands, there is none who seeks for God; all have turned aside, together they have become useless; there is none who does good, there is not even one. Their throat is an open grave, with their tongues they keep deceiving, the poison of asps is under their lips; whose mouth is full of cursing and bitterness; their feet are swift to shed blood, destruction and misery are in their paths, and the path of peace they have not known. There is no fear of God before their eyes."

Now we know that whatever the Law says, it speaks to those who are under the Law, so that every mouth may be closed and all the world may become accountable to God; because by the works of the Law no flesh will be justified in His sight; for through the Law comes the knowledge of sin.

FATHER, Your Word proves that the entire world is guilty before You. If left to ourselves, we would perish, as we deserve.
We are fallen human beings,
	and we therefore could never achieve righteousness through the law.

What the law *does* teach us is how how vile sin is,
>how hopelessly in bondage to evil we are,
>and how miserably worthy of judgment our sins have made us.

Holy God, we understand Your hatred for sin.
The law clearly manifests Your holy nature,
>leaving us stripped, barren, and guilty
>>so we can only run to You for mercy.
But Your Word bids us come boldly,
>and it reveals You to be a God of boundless compassion
>>and unfathomable grace
>>>who eagerly forgives all penitent, believing sinners.

Having been forgiven, we come before You now in prayer to adore You.
First we want to confess
>that although we are free from condemnation, we are still sinful.
We know that even our sins of thought,
>>evil desires, and other secret sins
>are not hidden from Your face, but are fully seen
>>by Your all-penetrating omniscience.[1]
We utterly abhor and renounce those evils.

Who is a God like You, who pardons iniquity?
What compassion You have had on us
>in treading all our iniquities under foot
>>and casting them into the depths of the sea![2]
We thank You, Lord, that the blood of Jesus Christ
>continually, faithfully, and justly cleanses us from our sins.[3]
Multiply Your grace in our lives.
Restrain our feet from evil;
>keep our lips from speaking falsely,
>and enable us to obey Your Word.

---

1. Psalm 90:8
2. Micah 7:18-19
3. 1 John 1:9

Set us free from slavery to corruption
    into the glorious liberty of the children of God.[1]

We know, Lord, that You have begun a good work in us
    and are faithfully continuing that work,
        which You will complete when we see our Lord Jesus face-to-face.[2]
We eagerly await that day.
Even so, Lord, come quickly!

Make us sensitive to the approach of sin and temptation.
Increase our loathing of all that is evil.
Heighten the godly fear that restrains our fleshly tendencies.
Overwhelm our hearts with the purifying power
    of Your Word and Your Spirit.
Fill us with compassion.
Perfect Your love in us.
Arouse in us a thirst for holiness.
Kindle a passion to serve You.
And lift us to higher worship.

May the words of our mouths and the meditation of our hearts
    be acceptable in Your sight, O Lord, our Rock and our Redeemer.[3]
In the name of our Lord Jesus Christ,
    who loved us and gave Himself for us, we pray—
    knowing that You hear
        and are always gracious to answer us. Amen.

---

1. Romans 8:21
2. Philippians 1:6; 1 John 3:2
3. Psalm 19:14

WEEK 40

IMITATING THE FAITH OF ABRAHAM

ROMANS 4:1-25

What then shall we say that Abraham, our forefather according to the flesh, has found? For if Abraham was justified by works, he has something to boast about, but not before God. For what does the Scripture say? "Abraham believed God, and it was credited to him as righteousness." Now to the one who works, his wage is not credited as a favor, but as what is due. But to the one who does not work, but believes in Him who justifies the ungodly, his faith is credited as righteousness, just as David also speaks of the blessing on the man to whom God credits righteousness apart from works: "Blessed are those whose lawless deeds have been forgiven, and whose sins have been covered. Blessed is the man whose sin the Lord will not take into account."

Is this blessing then on the circumcised, or on the uncircumcised also? For we say, "Faith was credited to Abraham as righteousness." How then was it credited? While he was circumcised, or uncircumcised? Not while circumcised, but while uncircumcised; and he received the sign of circumcision, a seal of the righteousness of the faith which he had while uncircumcised, so that he might be the father of all who believe without being circumcised, that righteousness might be credited to them, and the father of circumcision to those who not only are of the circumcision, but who also follow in the steps of the faith of our father Abraham which he had while uncircumcised.

For the promise to Abraham or to his descendants that he would be heir of the world was not through the Law, but through the righteousness of *faith. For if those who are of the Law are heirs, faith is made void and the promise is nullified; for the Law brings about wrath, but where there is no law, there also is no violation.*

For this reason it is by faith, in order that it may be in accordance with grace, so that the promise will be guaranteed to all the descendants, not only to those who are of the Law, but also to those who are of the faith of Abraham, who is the father of us all, (as it is written, "A father of many nations have I made you") in the presence of Him whom he believed, even God, who gives life to the dead and calls into being that which does not exist. In hope against hope he believed, so that he might become a father of many nations according to that which had been spoken, "So shall your descendants be." Without becoming weak in faith he contemplated his own body, now as good as dead since he was about a hundred years old, and the deadness of Sarah's womb; yet, with respect to the promise of God, he did not waver in unbelief but grew strong in faith, giving glory to God, and being fully assured that what God had promised, He was able also to perform. Therefore it was also credited to him as righteousness. Now not for his sake only was it written that it was credited to him, but for our sake also, to whom it will be credited, as those who believe in Him who raised Jesus our Lord from the dead, He who was delivered over because of our transgressions, and was raised because of our justification.

OUR FATHER, there are people who believe
> some ritual, rite, ceremony, or moral act
>> will earn righteousness and reconciliation with You,
>> but Your Word is clear: that belief is false.
We learn this especially from the example of Abraham,
> who received righteousness freely,
> by imputation from You,
> because he believed in the One who justifies the ungodly.

No one is godly apart from Your doing.

Abraham was blessed with the faith to take You at Your Word,
    and it was credited to him as righteousness
        before the rite of circumcision was established.[1]
Thus in the opening chapters of Genesis
    the way of salvation was set forth clearly for us.
It is always and only by grace through faith,
    lest anyone should boast.[2]

We acknowledge with gratitude that salvation is provided
    fully and freely by grace
        to those who put their faith in the Lord Jesus Christ.
Thank You for the grace that saves ungodly sinners like us
    who, left to ourselves and our own efforts,
    could never gain righteousness and would all perish in hell.
We come before You to celebrate Your grace
    in the power of the gospel,
    which has captured our souls for eternal life
        and our hearts for joyful worship.

So we come as undeserving sinners
    who have simply trusted Christ.
We look to Him alone for righteousness and reconciliation,
    fully realizing we have no capacity
        to satisfy Your holy standards on our own.

Work in us, we pray, a faith like Abraham's
    to take You at Your Word.
May it be steadfast and not marred by any doubts!
Confessing and setting aside our own sins and selves,
    we praise You for the greatness of
        Your mercy, grace, love, and pure goodness
            that will bring us to glory through Christ our Savior.
Receive our worship, for we bring it in His name. Amen.

---

1. Genesis 15:1-6, compared with Genesis 17:1-10
2. Ephesians 2:8-9

BEING IMITATORS
OF THE LORD

1 THESSALONIANS 1:1-10

Paul and Silvanus and Timothy,

To the church of the Thessalonians in God the Father and the Lord Jesus Christ: Grace to you and peace.

We give thanks to God always for all of you, making mention of you in our prayers; constantly bearing in mind your work of faith and labor of love and steadfastness of hope in our Lord Jesus Christ in the presence of our God and Father, knowing, brethren beloved by God, His choice of you; for our gospel did not come to you in word only, but also in power and in the Holy Spirit and with full conviction; just as you know what kind of men we proved to be among you for your sake. You also became imitators of us and of the Lord, having received the word in much tribulation with the joy of the Holy Spirit, so that you became an example to all the believers in Macedonia and in Achaia. For the word of the Lord has sounded forth from you, not only in Macedonia and Achaia, but also in every place your faith toward God has gone forth, so that we have no need to say anything. For they themselves report about us what kind of a reception we had with you, and how you turned to God from idols to serve a living and true God, and to wait for His Son from heaven, whom He raised from the dead, that is Jesus, who rescues us from the wrath to come.

FATHER, may our lives and our fellowship be marked by
    works of faith, labors of love, and steadfastness of hope.
By Your grace, we are holy people, beloved and chosen by You,
    and when the gospel came to us,
    it came not only in word but also in power,
    in the Holy Spirit, and with full conviction.
Not that we are sufficient in ourselves
    to claim anything as coming from us,
    but our sufficiency is from You.[1]
You are the one who accomplished our salvation,
    turning us from worldly things we once idolized
        to serve You, the living and true God.
You are the One who awakened us to receive Your Word—
    not as the word of men but for what it really is:
    the Word of God, which performs its perfect work
        in all who believe.[2]

So our salvation comes solely from You.
You sent Your Son to die for our sake
    while we were still sworn enemies of righteousness.[3]
You graciously removed the scales from our eyes and drew us to faith.
Open our eyes to see more of Your truth;
    open our hearts to believe it more earnestly;
    and open our mouths to declare it more faithfully.

May we be imitators of our Lord Jesus Christ
    and godly examples to one another.
Help us grow into full maturity and Christlikeness.
We know that the necessary nourishment
    for that kind of growth is found only in Your Word.[4]
We cannot thrive by bread alone,

1. 2 Corinthians 3:5
2. 1 Thessalonians 2:14
3. Romans 5:8
4. 1 Peter 2:2

but by every word that proceeds out of Your mouth.[1]

May we therefore search the Scriptures
    diligently and with singleness of heart,
    for in them we know we have eternal life.[2]
They point us to Christ.
They unveil His glory.
They reflect His holy character.
From them we learn of His suffering, death, resurrection, ascension,
    intercession, and glorious return.
By them You speak to us from heaven.
In them we hear the voice of the Spirit speaking plainly.

Give us attentive hearts.
Cause us to hear Your truth with all humility and obedience.
Open our eyes to see with clarity,
    and open our ears to hear with understanding.
May we heed every line with fear and trembling—
    not only the instructions, but also the reproofs;
    not only the promises, but also the threats.

We bless You that Your holy Word has been translated
    into our own language to show us the way of life.
May we never take that privilege for granted.
May we never neglect
    the rich counsel available to us on those pages.
May we drink deeply of its truth
    and feed our famished souls with its nourishment.

And may our hearts, like the hearts of those on the road to Emmaus,
    burn within us as You teach us.[3]
We pray in Jesus' name. Amen.

---

1. Matthew 4:4
2. John 5:39
3. Luke 24:13-35

LIVING A RADICALLY ALTERED LIFE

JAMES 2:14-26

What use is it, my brethren, if someone says he has faith but he has no works? Can that faith save him? If a brother or sister is without clothing and in need of daily food, and one of you says to them, "Go in peace, be warmed and be filled," and yet you do not give them what is necessary for their body, what use is that? Even so faith, if it has no works, is dead, being by itself.

But someone may well say, "You have faith and I have works; show me your faith without the works, and I will show you my faith by my works." You believe that God is one. You do well; the demons also believe, and shudder. But are you willing to recognize, you foolish fellow, that faith without works is useless? Was not Abraham our father justified by works when he offered up Isaac his son on the altar? You see that faith was working with his works, and as a result of the works, faith was perfected; and the Scripture was fulfilled which says, "And Abraham believed God, and it was reckoned to him as righteousness," and he was called the friend of God. You see that a man is justified by works and not by faith alone. In the same way, was not Rahab the harlot also justified by works when she received the messengers and sent them out by another way? For just as the body without the spirit is dead, so also faith without works is dead.

RIGHTEOUS LORD and sovereign Ruler of heaven and earth,
>   You have commissioned us to be witnesses,
>   taking the gospel of our Lord Jesus Christ into all the world.
Help us first and foremost to be faithful evangelists right where we are.
Make us effective heralds of your truth,
>   beginning in our own families and neighborhoods;
>   then extend our testimony in accord with Your plan—
>   even if that takes us to the uttermost parts of the world.

It is obvious that no one can put faith on display without works.
Our Lord Himself taught that every tree is known by its own fruit.[1]
We cannot rightly claim a faith that saves
>   when there is no evidence of
>   regeneration, conversion, transformation, or sanctification.
In that sense, the view from outside can be telling of what is inside.
Those who have been justified will act justly.

Yet we confess that we are *not* perfectly just.
We are fallen, error-prone, sinful creatures.
And yet, Lord, You have justified us
>   completely, instantaneously—
>   by imputing to us a perfect righteousness.
You credited us with merit that is not our own—
>   Christ's own spotless righteousness by faith.[2]
You don't count our transgressions against us.
And on that basis You have declared us altogether just.
Our reconciliation is complete.[3]
We are perfectly at peace with You.[4]
We face no condemnation in time or eternity.[5]

---

1. Luke 6:43-46
2. Philippians 3:9
3. 2 Corinthians 5:19
4. Romans 5:1
5. Romans 8:1

But You did not stop with our justification.

You did not merely forgive us and give us a right standing.

You also made us new creatures.[1]

How grateful we are for the total transformation
    of the inner man that has changed (and is still changing)
    our desires, attitudes, speech, and actions!

By the indwelling Holy Spirit
    we have not only a new desire for holiness
        but also a new power to pursue godly lives.[2]

The Spirit has given us new life,
    and He has placed a deep, sincere love in our hearts for You—
        and for our fellow believers.[3]

That love naturally manifests itself by Your grace.

And You give still *more* grace.

Though You resist the proud, You multiply grace to the humble.

Help us therefore to be humble, submissive, resistant
    to the wiles of Satan and the lure of this world.

Draw us near, cleanse our hands, purify our hearts,
    and give us single-minded devotion to Christ.[4]

Heavenly Father, continue shaping us into the people
    You want us to be so we can truly demonstrate to the world
    that the salvation You give is life-transforming.

May our radically altered lives
    give testimony to the power and glory of the gospel!

This we ask in the name of Christ Jesus our Lord. Amen.

---

1. 2 Corinthians 5:17-21
2. Philippians 2:13
3. Romans 5:5
4. James 4:6-8

WEEK 43

YEARNING TO BLESS GOD AND MAN

JAMES 3:1-12

Let not many of you become teachers, my brethren, knowing that as such we will incur a stricter judgment. For we all stumble in many ways. If anyone does not stumble in what he says, he is a perfect man, able to bridle the whole body as well. Now if we put the bits into the horses' mouths so that they will obey us, we direct their entire body as well. Look at the ships also, though they are so great and are driven by strong winds, are still directed by a very small rudder wherever the inclination of the pilot desires. So also the tongue is a small part of the body, and yet it boasts of great things.

See how great a forest is set aflame by such a small fire! And the tongue is a fire, the very world of iniquity; the tongue is set among our members as that which defiles the entire body, and sets on fire the course of our life, and is set on fire by hell. For every species of beasts and birds, of reptiles and creatures of the sea, is tamed and has been tamed by the human race. But no one can tame the tongue; it is a restless evil and full of deadly poison. With it we bless our Lord and Father, and with it we curse men, who have been made in the likeness of God; from the same mouth come both blessing and cursing. My brethren, these things ought not to be this way. Does a fountain send out from the same opening both fresh and bitter water? Can

a fig tree, my brethren, produce olives, or a vine produce figs? Nor can salt
water produce fresh.

DEAR LORD, as we now seek to bless You with our praise,
    we must confess that we are people with unclean lips.[1]
With the same tongue we use to bless You, Dear Father,
    we demean people who are made in Your image.
We acknowledge with deepest remorse
    that we are guilty of such gross hypocrisy,
        and it ought not to be this way.
We yearn rather to be characterized by speech
    that blesses You and edifies others.

So give us power and self-control
    to keep our tongues from evil
        and our lips from speaking deceit.[2]
Guard our ways that we may not sin with our tongues;
    guard our mouths as with a muzzle,
        especially when we are in the presence of the wicked.[3]
We know that by our words we will be justified,
    and by our words we will be condemned.[4]
So forgive us for the many ways we have sinned with our lips.
Sanctify our words to minister grace to the hearers.

In seeking Your forgiveness, we humbly acknowledge
    Your greatness, goodness, and unbounded kindness to us
        who trust in Christ Jesus.
We are bold to seek your mercy
    because You have revealed Yourself as a God

---

1. Isaiah 6:5
2. Psalm 34:13
3. Psalm 39:1
4. Matthew 12:37

who is longsuffering and kind,
ready and willing to pardon sin,
full of compassion and slow to anger.[1]
You comfort us in all our affliction,
and Your promises give us life and hope.[2]
On the basis of those promises, we turn to You for mercy and cleansing.

We declare with the psalmist that You,
Lord God, are a sun and shield;
You give grace and glory;
no good thing do You withhold
from those who walk uprightly.[3]
We bless You for exceedingly great and precious promises
that nourish us and comfort our souls,
yet we accept them not as mere comfort
but as encouragement and motivation
to a higher and more dedicated love
of godliness, obedience, and service.

Save us, we pray, from empty words
of praise and blessing given to You
and thoughtless, unkind, and cruel words
given to others who are made in Your image.
Give us by Your Holy Spirit control over our tongue,
which is supreme evidence of a disciplined life
under which all else is under control as well.
Grant us discipline of speech that comes from strength of character
so that out of the fountain of our lips
comes only that which is
sweet, fruitful, edifying,
uplifting, and Christ honoring.

---

1. Psalm 145:8
2. Psalm 119:49-50
3. Psalm 84:11-12

Fill us with grace that will make our speech always gracious.[1]
Forgive us for all our failures in speech,
    and make us clean again as we come into Your presence.
In our Savior's name we pray,
    asking that we learn to speak
        as graciously as He spoke. Amen.

---

1. Colossians 4:5-6

PRAYERS ON
USEFUL SERVICE

LONGING TO BE MORE USEFUL

1 John 4:1-10

Beloved, do not believe every spirit, but test the spirits to see whether they are from God, because many false prophets have gone out into the world. By this you know the Spirit of God: every spirit that confesses that Jesus Christ has come in the flesh is from God; and every spirit that does not confess Jesus is not from God; this is the spirit of the antichrist, of which you have heard that it is coming, and now it is already in the world.

You are from God, little children, and have overcome them; because greater is He who is in you than he who is in the world. They are from the world; therefore they speak as from the world, and the world listens to them. We are from God; he who knows God listens to us; he who is not from God does not listen to us. By this we know the spirit of truth and the spirit of error.

Beloved, let us love one another, for love is from God; and everyone who loves is born of God and knows God. The one who does not love does not know God, for God is love. By this the love of God was manifested in us, that God has sent His only begotten Son into the world so that we might live through Him. In this is love, not that we loved God, but that He loved us and sent His Son to be the propitiation for our sins.

GRACIOUS FATHER, we thank You for Your precious Word,
    which declares that Jesus Christ came in the flesh,
    and bore in His own body all our sins on the cross—
    thereby becoming the propitiation for those sins.
He satisfied justice, placated Your righteous wrath against sin,
    and fully canceled the certificate of debt
        consisting of decrees against us.
He took out of the way every element of the law that was hostile to us,
    nailing it to the cross.[1]
Then He rose as proof of our justification
    and future glorification in Your sight.[2]

Our guilt has therefore been put away forever.
Christ already bore our judgment,
    so there is no condemnation
        for those who are united with Christ by faith.[3]
We are dead to self, and our lives are hidden with Christ in You.[4]
Our full and free pardon is an accomplished fact.
Our lawless deeds are forgiven;
    our guilt is covered;
    and You do not count sin against us.[5]
That is Your just verdict from heaven's throne in our favor.

So we come to confess our sins not as legal transgressors
    who have been dragged before a judge,
        but as wayward children coming to a loving Father.
Although we have been justified
    and washed from our sins in the eternal sense,
        we still need daily cleansing, fatherly correction,
        and restored communion with You.

1. Colossians 2:14
2. Romans 1:1-4; 8:28-30
3. Romans 8:1
4. Colossians 3:3
5. Romans 4:7-8

So forgive us, dear Father, for sins of rebellion—
>   those times when we have knowingly disobeyed
>   Your commandments.
Forgive us for other sins of commission:
>   foolish sins, worldly lusts,
>   evil thoughts, and wicked pride.
We are also guilty of many sins of omission:
>   we have shirked our duties,
>   neglected the needs of our neighbors,
>   squandered opportunities to do good,
>   and failed to render appropriate worship and service to You.

When we stumble and are weak,
>   when we sin, when we are negligent in praise
>   or careless in our thoughts, it grieves us.
We see the wretchedness of sin. We feel the shame of it.
We can only begin to see how much our sin cost Christ.
We bless You that the atonement He made
>   is so wonderfully and completely sufficient.

We trust that You, O God,
>   through the power of Your Spirit who indwells us,
>   will sanctify us.
Help us recognize, despise, and mortify the sin that remains.
When we stray, arrest our hearts.
Convict us, awaken our consciences,
>   and draw us back to Your throne of grace.
May we be thorough and sincere in every confession,
>   and may we henceforth be more faithful—
>   and thus more useful.
Empower us by Your Spirit and order our steps
>   according to Your Word.

This we pray in the name of Christ. Amen.

WEEK 45

SEEKING TO BE A BLESSING

GALATIANS 6:1-18

Brethren, even if anyone is caught in any trespass, you who are spiritual, restore such a one in a spirit of gentleness; each one looking to yourself, so that you too will not be tempted. Bear one another's burdens, and thereby fulfill the law of Christ. For if anyone thinks he is something when he is nothing, he deceives himself. But each one must examine his own work, and then he will have reason for boasting in regard to himself alone, and not in regard to another. For each one will bear his own load.

The one who is taught the word is to share all good things with the one who teaches him.

Do not be deceived, God is not mocked; for whatever a man sows, this he will also reap. For the one who sows to his own flesh will from the flesh reap corruption, but the one who sows to the Spirit will from the Spirit reap eternal life. Let us not lose heart in doing good, for in due time we will reap if we do not grow weary.

So then, while we have opportunity, let us do good to all people, and especially to those who are of the household of the faith.

See with what large letters I am writing to you with my own hand. Those who desire to make a good showing in the flesh try to compel you to be circumcised, simply so that they will not be persecuted for the cross of Christ. For those who are circumcised do not even keep the Law themselves, but they desire to have you circumcised so that they may boast in your flesh.

But may it never be that I would boast, except in the cross of our Lord

Jesus Christ, through which the world has been crucified to me, and I to the world. For neither is circumcision anything, nor uncircumcision, but a new creation. And those who will walk by this rule, peace and mercy be upon them, and upon the Israel of God.

From now on let no one cause trouble for me, for I bear on my body the brand-marks of Jesus. The grace of our Lord Jesus Christ be with your spirit, brethren. Amen.

THANK YOU, LORD, for calling us into Your kingdom and family.
Two of our responsibilities as family are to restore with humility
    those who have been caught in sin's web, and
        to help carry one another's burdens.
In such actions, we fulfill the royal law of Christ,
    which is distilled in the principle of love.[1]
We recognize that all the moral duties Your law sets forth
    are precisely the same virtues that arise out of authentic love.
May we be faithful vessels of the love
    Your Spirit sheds abroad in our hearts.[2]
May we never be guilty of hiding
    the light of Your love under a bushel.[3]

Your Word often reminds us of the inexorable law of sowing and reaping.
Whatever we sow we reap, spiritually as well as physically.
May we always sow to the Spirit and not to the flesh!
We confess that we cannot do that
    without Your gracious enablement,
    and so we seek the aid of Your Spirit.

You have also taught us that the one who sows sparingly
        will reap sparingly,

1. James 2:8
2. Romans 5:5
3. Matthew 5:15

and the one who sows bountifully
    will reap bountifully.[1]
May we always be liberal and open-handed
    in the sowing of good things.
We're reminded especially of our duty to share in all good things
    with those who have taught us the Word.
Fill us with gratitude and with generosity;
    then open our hearts to be channels of blessing,
    especially to those who have so wonderfully blessed us.

Help us to be both wise and aggressive in taking advantage
    of the opportunities we have to do good to all,
    especially our own dear brothers and sisters in Christ.
Harness our gifts and abilities—
    along with all our human faculties—
    and employ them for Your glory.
Empower us to work harder, serve more faithfully,
    labor more diligently, and still press on—
    even when the trials and distractions of this life
        seem to offer compelling motives
            to turn away from the needs of others.
Energize us by Your Spirit and keep us faithful to our calling.

You know, dear Lord, that our lives here on earth
    are full of burdens, heartaches, and disappointments.
You permit those things to use them for our benefit.
May we bear them with grace and courage.
We thank You for the grace that sustains us
    in the midst of all our troubles.
We pray that through the trials You send our way
    You will keep our hearts filled
        with that peace which surpasses all comprehension

---

1. 2 Corinthians 9:6

and guards our hearts and minds in Christ Jesus.[1]

Thank You that when we falter or fail,
    You always restore us.
You give us grace upon grace without measure.
You abundantly supply every need we have.

But we confess, Lord, that one of our greatest needs is for holiness.
We are prone to sin, predisposed to folly,
    given to stubbornness, and easily confounded
        by our own self-will.
Guide, guard, and sustain us to keep our feet from slipping,
    and keep us ever mindful of—and firmly anchored to—
    the solid foundation You have given us in Christ.

Give us a greater love for Him,
    so that all our service flows from hearts of gladness.
Give us a holy longing to be free from sin
    in both mind and action.
Whether Your plan for our immediate future entails
        prosperity or adversity,
        blessing or suffering,
        joy or sorrow—
        or a loving mixture of all those things—
prepare us to respond with uprightness of heart
        and Christlike holiness.
Your grace is sufficient for all these things,
    and Your truth strengthens us for all things.

We bow our hearts to worship You
    in Your Son's blessed name. Amen.

---

1. Philippians 4:6-7

BEING EMPOWERED
TO SERVE

ROMANS 6:11-23

E*ven so consider yourselves to be dead to sin, but alive to God in Christ Jesus. Therefore do not let sin reign in your mortal body so that you obey its lusts, and do not go on presenting the members of your body to sin as instruments of unrighteousness; but present yourselves to God as those alive from the dead, and your members as instruments of righteousness to God. For sin shall not be master over you, for you are not under law but under grace.*

What then? Shall we sin because we are not under law but under grace? May it never be! Do you not know that when you present yourselves to someone as slaves for obedience, you are slaves of the one whom you obey, either of sin resulting in death, or of obedience resulting in righteousness?

But thanks be to God that though you were slaves of sin, you became obedient from the heart to that form of teaching to which you were committed, and having been freed from sin, you became slaves of righteousness. I am speaking in human terms because of the weakness of your flesh. For just as you presented your members as slaves to impurity and to lawlessness, resulting in further lawlessness, so now present your members as slaves to righteousness, resulting in sanctification.

For when you were slaves of sin, you were free in regard to righteousness. Therefore what benefit were you then deriving from the things of which you are now ashamed? For the outcome of those things is death. But now having been freed from sin and enslaved to God, you derive your benefit, resulting

in sanctification, and the outcome, eternal life. For the wages of sin is death,
but the free gift of God is eternal life in Christ Jesus our Lord.

HEAVENLY FATHER, how grateful we are
    that the reign of sin is ended in our lives!
We are no longer slaves to iniquity and unrighteousness
    but we are *Your* slaves—slaves to righteousness.
What dominates us now is no longer sin, but righteousness.
Your Son shed His own blood
    to purchase us out of sin's slave-market,
    and now we belong to You—
    body, soul, spirit, heart, mind, will, and affections.
Use our every faculty for Your glory;
    make us profitable servants;
    employ us as unashamed workmen—
    envoys and ambassadors
        for the expansion of Your kingdom and glory.

O Father, our hearts overflow with joy and gratitude
    because we have been regenerated.
Our hearts have been totally renewed.
We have been made completely new creatures in Christ.
Nevertheless, in this earthly life we still face
    the presence of remaining sin in our flesh.
And it must be subdued.

Give us the strength and a heartfelt willingness—
    by the power of Your Spirit—
    to mortify the sin in our members
        day by day,
        hour by hour,
        moment by moment.

Give us such a love for Christ
and a devotion to virtue and holiness
that we will gladly yield ourselves
as dutiful servants to righteousness.
Our desire is to participate in the full blessedness of sanctification
and to bring honor to Your name—
at home, in Your church,
in the workplace, in our communities,
and wherever else You might send us.

Help us to do all our work with excellence,
in Your sight as well as in the eyes of others.
Remind us each moment to give You glory
even in the smallest, most mundane activities of life.[1]
Teach us to number our days
so that we will apply our hearts to wisdom.[2]
Make us careful how we walk,
not as unwise men but as wise, making the most of our time—
because not only do we know our time is short;
but we also sense that these are evil times.[3]

When high unemployment and other economic,
political, or social difficulties trouble our land,
help us not to fear, but to trust in Your provision.
We trust that You will not only meet our needs,
but also give us enough to share with others in need.
May we never close up our hearts of compassion against them.[4]

We know, dear Lord, that all who live faithfully in Christ
will suffer persecution.[5]

---

1. Ephesians 6:5-8; 1 Corinthians 10:31
2. Psalm 90:12
3. Ephesians 5:15-17
4. 1 John 3:17
5. 2 Timothy 3:12

The occasional taunts and harassments we face
    are blessedly mild by comparison
        to the suffering and deaths of so many saints
            who have gone before us.
May we never grow complacent
    or so accustomed to the comforts of our culture's apathy
        that we lose our boldness.
Above all, may we not yearn for worldly approval.
We know that it would be the very height of infidelity
    to seek accolades from the same world that hated Christ.[1]
Help us to be faithful, and may we (like Christ)
    simply scorn worldly shame
        for the sake of the joy set before us.[2]

We thank You, Lord, that although the wages of sin is death,
    we have received salvation freely.
Eternal life is ours in Christ Jesus our Lord—
    at the highest imaginable cost to Him,
    but without money and without price to us.[3]
Our present and our future are secure.
Our eternity is unimaginably rich
    with blessings that no one can ever take from us.

Help us to honor our Savior in our worship.
We bring all these prayers before You
    in His holy name. Amen.

1. John 15:18-19
2. Hebrews 12:2
3. Isaiah 55:1

DESIRING TO BE ACCEPTABLE

1 Corinthians 6:12-20

*A*ll things are lawful for me, but not all things are profitable. All things are lawful for me, but I will not be mastered by anything. Food is for the stomach and the stomach is for food, but God will do away with both of them. Yet the body is not for immorality, but for the Lord, and the Lord is for the body.

Now God has not only raised the Lord, but will also raise us up through His power. Do you not know that your bodies are members of Christ? Shall I then take away the members of Christ and make them members of a prostitute? May it never be! Or do you not know that the one who joins himself to a prostitute is one body with her? For He says, "The two shall become one flesh." But the one who joins himself to the Lord is one spirit with Him.

Flee immorality. Every other sin that a man commits is outside the body, but the immoral man sins against his own body. Or do you not know that your body is a temple of the Holy Spirit who is in you, whom you have from God, and that you are not your own? For you have been bought with a price: therefore glorify God in your body.

OUR FATHER, we thank You for the joyous anticipation we have
of heaven and the incomparable realities
that are being prepared for us in glory.

May our hearts always be eager
>   for the eternal blessedness that awaits us in heaven.
Our highest hopes are fixed there;
>   may our daily thoughts be focused there as well.[1]
In the meantime, may we be faithful
>   to render our spiritual duty here in this earthly life:
>   May we earnestly present ourselves as living sacrifices to You.[2]

We come before You now as living stones, active building-blocks,
>   a spiritual house You are constructing—
>   the spiritual temple for a holy priesthood,
>   to offer up spiritual sacrifices
>>   acceptable to You through Jesus Christ.
You have made us a chosen race,
>>   a royal priesthood, a holy nation,
>>   a people for Your own possession
>   so that we may proclaim Your excellencies.[3]

The sacrifices of the Old Covenant were dead animals,
>   but Christ established the New Covenant
>>   through the all-sufficient sacrifice of Himself.
The animal sacrifices were merely symbols,
>   because it is impossible for the blood of bulls and goats
>>   to take away sins.[4]
But Christ offered one fully efficacious sacrifice for sins forever,
>   and then He sat down at Your right hand.[5]
Now it is our privilege and our duty
>   to offer *ourselves* to Him.

---

1. Colossians 3:2
2. Romans 12:1
3. 1 Peter 2:5,9
4. Hebrews 10:4
5. Hebrews 10:12

We are grateful to have gifts that differ
    according to the grace given us.
Help us to exercise them accordingly.[1]
Help us each to fulfill the role You have given us in the Body,
    so that the church can be stronger and manifest more powerfully
        the honor of Christ to a watching world.
Remind us and empower us to encourage and stimulate one another
    to love and good deeds.[2]

Thank You, precious Lord, for all Your mercies.
Not only do we not know how to pray as we ought;[3]
    human language does not possess words sufficient
        to praise You as You deserve.
You alone are Lord.
You made the heavens and all their host.
You set the universe in motion.
You formed the earth and all that is in it.
You made the seas and all that is in them.
You give life to all of them,
    and the heavenly host bows down before You.
You are the Lord God, who chose Abram and brought him out
    from Ur of the Chaldees.[4]
You also chose us and appointed us to go and bear fruit,
    and You ordained that our fruit would remain.

Apart from the life of Your Spirit in us,
    we would be utterly fruitless.
Enable us by grace to abide in Christ,
    that the life of His Spirit may flow through us.

---

1. Romans 12:6-8
2. Hebrews 10:24
3. Romans 8:26
4. Nehemiah 9:6

And may the result be an abundance of fruit—
all to Your glory and for Your good pleasure.
Help us, like Christ, always to do the things
that are pleasing to You.[1]

Above all, may we flee immorality and other sins of the body.
We know that we are not our own;
we have been bought at an unthinkably high price.
Help us, therefore, to glorify You in our bodies.

Give us great joy among Your people and a renewed love for You, Father,
as we present these requests in the name of Jesus Christ. Amen.

---

1. John 8:29

WEEK 48

REJOICING TO HAVE A
PIECE OF GOD'S ACTION

ROMANS 15:15-33

I have written very boldly to you on some points so as to remind you again, because of the grace that was given me from God, to be a minister of Christ Jesus to the Gentiles, ministering as a priest the gospel of God, so that my offering of the Gentiles may become acceptable, sanctified by the Holy Spirit. Therefore in Christ Jesus I have found reason for boasting in things pertaining to God.

For I will not presume to speak of anything except what Christ has accomplished through me, resulting in the obedience of the Gentiles by word and deed, in the power of signs and wonders, in the power of the Spirit; so that from Jerusalem and round about as far as Illyricum I have fully preached the gospel of Christ. And thus I aspired to preach the gospel, not where Christ was already named, so that I would not build on another man's foundation; but as it is written, "They who had no news of him shall see, and they who have not heard shall understand."

For this reason I have often been prevented from coming to you; but now, with no further place for me in these regions, and since I have had for many years a longing to come to you whenever I go to Spain—for I hope to see you in passing, and to be helped on my way there by you, when I have first enjoyed your company for a while—but now, I am going to Jerusalem serving the saints. For Macedonia and Achaia have been pleased to make a contribution for the poor among the saints in Jerusalem. Yes, they were pleased to do so, and they are indebted to them. For if the Gentiles have *shared in their spiritual things, they are indebted to minister to them also in material things.*

Therefore, when I have finished this, and have put my seal on this fruit of theirs, I will go on by way of you to Spain. I know that when I come to you, I will come in the fullness of the blessing of Christ.

Now I urge you, brethren, by our Lord Jesus Christ and by the love of the Spirit, to strive together with me in your prayers to God for me, that I may be rescued from those who are disobedient in Judea, and that my service for Jerusalem may prove acceptable to the saints; so that I may come to you in joy by the will of God and find refreshing rest in your company. Now the God of peace be with you all. Amen.

OUR FATHER, we are reminded often in Your Word
   that although the great work of redemption
      is a sovereign work done by Your will and power,
      not by the will and power of man,
      still You have graciously determined
         to use human instruments in carrying out
            Your redemptive work.
We see that plainly in the life of Your faithful servant Paul,
      in all the ways he set his life apart to be used,
      all the plans he made,
      all the letters he wrote,
      all the truths he expounded,
      all the places he visited,
      all the people he influenced,
   and his tremendous sense of vision, hope,
      and anticipation for the future.
Here was a man who rejoiced at the privilege
      of fitting into Your plans and was obviously thrilled
         to have a piece of the divine action!

Once redeemed, Paul had no interest whatsoever
    in trying to make You fit
        into his own feeble plans, ideas, or aspirations.

We see in Paul's example the mind of Christ in action.
Your own precious Son, co-equal and co-eternal with You,
    did not regard equality with God a thing to be grasped,
    but emptied Himself,
    taking a position of abject slavery as a true man,
    subject to all the same infirmities that trouble us.
Then He further humbled Himself
    by becoming obedient to the point of death—
    even death on a cross.[1]
Give us a similar perspective on life and ministry.
May we be humble, self-sacrificial, faithful servants
    to the needs of others rather than merely seekers of self-interest.

We confess, dear Lord, that we have failed miserably
    to follow the example Christ set for us.
We give in too easily to temptation.
We think too highly of ourselves.
We sacrifice too little for others.
We invest too much time in trivial and worldly pursuits.
Move our hearts to devote more time to worship and prayer.
Purge our minds not only from evil thoughts and sinful desires,
    but also from worthless and inconsequential matters.
May all our resources be devoted to Your honor
    and the pursuit of Your kingdom.
Let nothing hinder our worship and service
    for our Savior's sake.

Lift up the light of Your countenance upon us, O Lord!
You have put gladness in our hearts.[2]

---

1. Philippians 2:6-8
2. Psalm 4:6-7

You have graced us with a peace
    that passes human understanding.[1]
You make us sing for joy.
You shelter us beneath Your wings.
You surround us with favor and blessing.[2]
How majestic is Your name in all the earth![3]

We present our hearts, our minds,
    our tongues, our hands and feet—
    our every faculty—
    to You as a living sacrifice of praise.
We know, dear Lord, that even if we were able perfectly to devote
        every ounce of our energy,
        every molecule of our flesh,
        every moment of our time,
        every thought of our hearts,
        and every breath of our remaining lives to You in praise,
    it would not be sufficient to express even the tiniest fraction
        of Your glory.
That's why we look forward to an eternity of praising You
    in the perfect bliss of heaven.

In the meantime, enlarge our capacity for praise.
Open our eyes to behold Your glory more clearly
    than we see it now.
Open our hearts to love You more earnestly
    than we love anything in this world.
Open our tongues to praise You more fittingly
    than we can through these poor words.

We ask these things in the blessed name of Your Son,
    our Savior, the Lord Jesus Christ. Amen.

---

1. Philippians 4:7
2. Psalm 5:11-12
3. Psalm 8:9

PRESENTING OURSELVES AS A LIVING SACRIFICE

Romans 16:1-16

I commend to you our sister Phoebe, who is a servant of the church which is at Cenchrea; that you receive her in the Lord in a manner worthy of the saints, and that you help her in whatever matter she may have need of you; for she herself has also been a helper of many, and of myself as well.

Greet Prisca and Aquila, my fellow workers in Christ Jesus, who for my life risked their own necks, to whom not only do I give thanks, but also all the churches of the Gentiles; also greet the church that is in their house. Greet Epaenetus, my beloved, who is the first convert to Christ from Asia. Greet Mary, who has worked hard for you. Greet Andronicus and Junias, my kinsmen and my fellow prisoners, who are outstanding among the apostles, who also were in Christ before me. Greet Ampliatus, my beloved in the Lord. Greet Urbanus, our fellow worker in Christ, and Stachys my beloved. Greet Apelles, the approved in Christ. Greet those who are of the household of Aristobulus. Greet Herodion, my kinsman.

Greet those of the household of Narcissus, who are in the Lord. Greet Tryphaena and Tryphosa, workers in the Lord. Greet Persis the beloved, who has worked hard in the Lord. Greet Rufus, a choice man in the Lord, also his mother and mine. Greet Asyncritus, Phlegon, Hermes, Patrobas, Hermas and the brethren with them. Greet Philologus and Julia, Nereus and his sister, and Olympas, and all the saints who are with them. Greet one another with a holy kiss. All the churches of Christ greet you.

❄

OUR FATHER, thank You that You have
    designed a plan of redemption
    that rescues the unworthy and the guilty from their plight
        and places them into Your kingdom.
That kingdom exists not only as a heavenly, eternal realm;
    it also has a vital presence now on this earth.
We rejoice that You design to build Your kingdom
    through Your Body, the church,
        every member having an important part to play.

Thinking of the apostle Paul, we recognize the unique gifts and abilities
    he was given to advance Your kingdom,
        yet we are greatly encouraged to realize
            that the Holy Scriptures honor by name
                those who helped him.
You surrounded Paul with people we would not know
    had he not named those who prayed for him,
    encouraged him, and assisted him in Your great work.

Thank You, Lord, for such an example
    of the Body of Christ working together.
We are reminded that You not only save sinners;
    You also bring them together in one Body
        under the power of Your Spirit
            to accomplish Your glorious purposes.
Your grace is abundant in every way.
We bless You for the gospel and all that it brings:
    salvation,
    liberation,
    healing,
    wholeness,
    and hope.

Thank You that You equip us and blend us together
    in this wonderful entity called the Body of Christ.

We confess there are times
    when we are not useful as we should be—
    and sometimes we are even a hindrance to Your work.
We grieve the Holy Spirit. We seek the pleasures of the world.
We live without heed to our duties. We trifle with things that are evil.

We confess, moreover, that we are at times
    unloving, uncaring, proud, selfish, impatient, too earthly minded,
    and too apathetic about the things that really matter.
How desperately we need to come before You
    to be washed and forgiven of all such things.
May we mortify our sins at their first appearance
    and never let them linger!
Our heartfelt desire is to manifest Christ in His great glory.
We are the Body of which He is Head.
May we honor Him accordingly in everything we do and teach.

In all the ways we have offended You, Lord,
    we humbly ask for Your pardon.
How grateful we are that You are willing to forgive repentant sinners
    and restore us for useful service!
Our earnest desire is to be suitable instruments in Your hands.
May we be faithful in Your service.
Enlarge our capacity for gospel work,
    and intensify the reflection of Your glory on our faces.

You, Lord, are everything we need;
    may we desire nothing more.
You are our stronghold and our Deliverer.
You are our strength and our hope.
You are our Guide and our Keeper.
You are the one true God, and the Rock of our salvation.

All Your grace abounds to us;
    we always have full sufficiency in everything.
Indeed, we have an abundance for every good deed.[1]
May we not squander such exquisite blessings.

Cleanse us, so that we might more clearly reflect
    the glory of Christ.
Help us, even now, to give more perfect expression
    to the praise that will occupy our hearts throughout all eternity.
As always, we bring all these petitions in His blessed name.
May they be heard and answered
    as they are consistent with Your will. Amen.

1. 2 Corinthians 9:8

CARRYING OUT THE GREAT COMMISSION

MATTHEW 28

Now after the Sabbath, as it began to dawn toward the first day of the week, Mary Magdalene and the other Mary came to look at the grave. And behold, a severe earthquake had occurred, for an angel of the Lord descended from heaven and came and rolled away the stone and sat upon it. And his appearance was like lightning, and his clothing as white as snow. The guards shook for fear of him and became like dead men.

The angel said to the women, "Do not be afraid; for I know that you are looking for Jesus who has been crucified. He is not here, for He has risen, just as He said. Come, see the place where He was lying. Go quickly and tell His disciples that He has risen from the dead; and behold, He is going ahead of you into Galilee, there you will see Him; behold, I have told you."

And they left the tomb quickly with fear and great joy and ran to report it to His disciples. And behold, Jesus met them and greeted them. And they came up and took hold of His feet and worshiped Him. Then Jesus said to them, "Do not be afraid; go and take word to My brethren to leave for Galilee, and there they will see Me."

Now while they were on their way, some of the guard came into the city and reported to the chief priests all that had happened. And when they had assembled with the elders and consulted together, they gave a large sum of money to the soldiers, and said, "You are to say, 'His disciples came by night and stole Him away while we were asleep.' And if this should come to the governor's ears, we will win him over and keep you out of trouble." And *they took the money and did as they had been instructed; and this story was widely spread among the Jews, and is to this day.*

But the eleven disciples proceeded to Galilee, to the mountain which Jesus had designated. When they saw Him, they worshiped Him; but some were doubtful. And Jesus came up and spoke to them, saying, "All authority has been given to Me in heaven and on earth. Go therefore and make disciples of all the nations, baptizing them in the name of the Father and the Son and the Holy Spirit, teaching them to observe all that I commanded you; and lo, I am with you always, even to the end of the age."

GRACIOUS FATHER, our hearts are filled with praise.
The resurrection of Christ is the high point of all history.
It is the proof of our justification;
    the heart of the gospel message,
    the ground of our hope for eternal life,
    and the living guarantee of Christ's ultimate triumph
        over evil and all its consequences.

Your commission to us is unmistakable as well,
    for our risen Lord and Savior,
    the One to whom all authority in heaven and on earth
        has been given,
    has outlined the strategy from now to the end of the age
        with that one simple command:
            Go and make disciples,
                teaching them the full counsel of Your truth.
May we personally embrace His call, beginning where we are.
And may the gospel go forth with power and clarity into all nations.

Help us to be disciple-makers.
Empower us to use whatever gifts You have given us
    for the fulfillment of the task Christ set before His apostles.

May we ourselves be faithful not only to teach others
>   but also to obey from the heart everything He has commanded.

We long to see Your kingdom infiltrate and ultimately overcome
>   every place where Satan currently reigns.
We long to see the saving power of the gospel
>   unleashed to the uttermost parts of the earth.
We long to see Your glory and honor proclaimed among the nations.
May we earnestly embrace
>   whatever aspect of the task You have called us to,
>   and may we never shirk the duty or neglect an opportunity
>   to be heralds of the good news in whatever realm
>   You have placed us.

We cling to the promise of Christ that He will be present with us,
>   even to the end of the age.
We know that He will never leave us or forsake us.
That alone is good reason for us
>   to be free from all covetousness
>   and fully satisfied with whatever we have.[1]

We pray, dear Lord, that You might use us
>   to bring Your love and forgiveness to those around us
>   who so desperately need You.
We know that You rejoice in the salvation of sinners.
Indeed, all the inhabitants of heaven celebrate
>   when sinners are rescued and lives are redeemed.[2]
May redemption therefore be the central theme of *our* lives.

Do what You will to make us more effective ambassadors
>   for Your kingdom.
Mold our lives, our words, our actions toward others,
>   and even our thoughts to make us useful and effective evangelists,

1. Hebrews 13:5
2. Luke 15:1-32

reaching out to souls who are perishing all around us—
snatching them from the flames.[1]

Let us be willing to live and die to that end.
Cleanse us thoroughly from sin,
    and make us vessels fit for Your use.
Fill us with your Spirit;
    unleash Your truth in our hearts;
    sanctify us by Your Word;
    embolden us with Your power;
    give us empathy with the plight of those in bondage to sin;
    and help us to declare the way of salvation
        in a way that draws men and women to Christ.
All these things we pray in Jesus' blessed name. Amen.

1. Jude 23

CONTEMPLATING THE POWER OF THE CHURCH

EPHESIANS 4:1-16

Therefore I, the prisoner of the Lord, implore you to walk in a manner worthy of the calling with which you have been called, with all humility and gentleness, with patience, showing tolerance for one another in love, being diligent to preserve the unity of the Spirit in the bond of peace.

There is one body and one Spirit, just as also you were called in one hope of your calling; one Lord, one faith, one baptism, one God and Father of all who is over all and through all and in all. But to each one of us grace was given according to the measure of Christ's gift. Therefore it says, "When He ascended on high, He led captive a host of captives, and He gave gifts to men." (Now this expression, "He ascended," what does it mean except that He also had descended into the lower parts of the earth? He who descended is Himself also He who ascended far above all the heavens, so that He might fill all things.)

And He gave some as apostles, and some as prophets, and some as evangelists, and some as pastors and teachers, for the equipping of the saints for the work of service, to the building up of the body of Christ; until we all attain to the unity of the faith, and of the knowledge of the Son of God, to a mature man, to the measure of the stature which belongs to the fullness of Christ.

As a result, we are no longer to be children, tossed here and there by waves and carried about by every wind of doctrine, by the trickery of men, *by craftiness in deceitful scheming; but speaking the truth in love, we are to grow up in all aspects into Him who is the head, even Christ, from whom the whole body, being fitted and held together by what every joint supplies, according to the proper working of each individual part, causes the growth of the body for the building up of itself in love.*

FATHER, through the years as we have
    followed Christ, we have observed
    (and in some measure experienced)
    how His church is fitted and held together organically
        as a single body, according to the proper working of each part
            by the power of the Holy Spirit.
We have witnessed the growth of the Body as it is built up in love.
We ourselves are members of that one Body—
    the true church consisting of all the redeemed.
We believe in one Holy Spirit,
    who indwells us both individually and collectively,
    the divine Source of our life and power.
We trust in one hope—one way to heaven—
    because we know there is just one Lord, one faith, one baptism,
    and one God and Father over all.

As we endeavor to sustain our unity in the bond of peace,
    at the same time we thank You
        for the diversity that exists in the Body.
You have given separate gifts to each of us that blend wonderfully together,
    like ingredients in a delicious recipe,
    so that the Body wonderfully manifests the true beauty of Christ.

We long that Christ be on full display through us as His Body!
We have no desire for the praise and honor of this world.

We have no esteem for superficial and ceremonial
    religious accomplishments.
We have no regard for works done
    primarily to be seen by other people.
We desire rather that Your Spirit would have His way in our hearts.
The spiritual treasures we possess
    have been bestowed upon frail earthen vessels
        so that what shines through
            obviously comes from You and not ourselves.[1]
Your strength is thus made perfect through our weakness;[2]
    and Your glory is thereby put on display in us.
What an unspeakable privilege that is for redeemed sinners such as we are!

Thank You for sermons and other Bible lessons
    that accurately convey Your Holy Word
        and serve as means of grace that enable us to experience
            Your truth, power, and love.
Our Lord Jesus said You are glorified when we bear much fruit;
    therefore we ask that our hearts would be good soil
        that receives the seed of Your Word
            by hearing, accepting, understanding, and obeying it.[3]

Your Word has dispelled our doubts,
    diminished our discouragements,
    convicted us, confronted us, humbled us,
    and kept us from any sense of self-importance.
Pour out Your blessings on our labors in Your name,
    and help us to function in Your strength.
Pour out Your power on Your people,
    and may Your church be faithful and fruitful
        in proclaiming the message of salvation.

---

1. 2 Corinthians 4:7,15-17
2. 2 Corinthians 12:9
3. John 15:8; Matthew 13:23; Mark 4:20

We are privileged and humbled
>   to be counted as Your fellow workers.
Give us faithful, devoted hearts.
May we be true to Your plan for the church;
>   keep us ever mindful to take care how we build
>   on that exquisite foundation that was laid in the apostolic era.[1]

Incline our hearts to Your truth.
Guide our steps as we seek to walk in all Your ways
>   and obey all Your commandments.
Hear these requests, we pray in Jesus' name.
And may all the peoples of the earth know
>   that You are God; there is no other.[2] Amen.

---

1. 1 Corinthians 3:9-10
2. 1 Kings 8:58-60

LIVING A TRANSFORMED LIFE

JAMES 2:1-13

My brethren, do not hold your faith in our glorious Lord Jesus Christ with an attitude of personal favoritism. For if a man comes into your assembly with a gold ring and dressed in fine clothes, and there also comes in a poor man in dirty clothes, and you pay special attention to the one who is wearing the fine clothes, and say, "You sit here in a good place," and you say to the poor man, "You stand over there, or sit down by my footstool," have you not made distinctions among yourselves, and become judges with evil motives?

Listen, my beloved brethren: did not God choose the poor of this world to be rich in faith and heirs of the kingdom which He promised to those who love Him? But you have dishonored the poor man. Is it not the rich who oppress you and personally drag you into court? Do they not blaspheme the fair name by which you have been called?

If, however, you are fulfilling the royal law according to the Scripture, "You shall love your neighbor as yourself," you are doing well. But if you show partiality, you are committing sin and are convicted by the law as transgressors. For whoever keeps the whole law and yet stumbles in one point, he has become guilty of all. For He who said, "Do not commit adultery," also said, "Do not commit murder." Now if you do not commit adultery, but do commit murder, you have become a transgressor of the law.

So speak and so act as those who are to be judged by the law of liberty.
For judgment will be merciless to one who has shown no mercy; mercy tri-
umphs over judgment.

ALMIGHTY GOD, we are privileged to call You *our* Father.
   You loved us and saved us and adopted us
         into Your own family.
You have therefore called us as believers
   to love one another with pure hearts fervently. [1]
That includes not showing partiality,
   which is one important way of fulfilling the royal law
         of loving our neighbors as ourselves.
Help us abound in love,
   and keep us from making ungodly distinctions
         between one another.
May our actions toward one another reflect the perfect love
   with which You first loved us.

We take to heart how Christ taught us to pray,
   yearning for Your name to be hallowed,
   Your kingdom to come,
   and Your will to be done on earth as it is in heaven.
Those are the true desires of our hearts;
   forgive us for being so preoccupied with lesser things.

And yet You also invite us to ask You for our temporal needs—
   our daily bread and other needs, all of which You richly supply.
Always You answer with surpassingly more abundance
   than we have faith to ask or think. [2]

---

1. 1 Peter 1:22
2. Ephesians 3:20

We drink our fill of that abundance;
 and You keep it flowing like a river.
For with You is the fountain of life; in Your light we see light.[1]
May we never forget how dependent we are
 on Your generous bounty;
 give us truly grateful hearts, and fill our mouths with praise.

How thankful we are for the written Word—
 that razor-sharp two-edged sword,
 which is able to discern our thoughts and intentions[2]
  even more accurately than we can know our own hearts.[3]
The Word cleanses and sanctifies us.[4]
It gives understanding to our minds,
 wisdom to our thoughts, and light to our path.[5]
It is perfect, utterly transfiguring our inmost beings.[6]
May our lives—like the apostles'—
 be so evidently transformed by Your truth
  that people will take note that we have been with Jesus.[7]

You, our great Redeemer, have led us out of the desert of sin
 into a flourishing place of righteousness.
Lead us into a still-wider garden of holiness
 so that we can fully enjoy
 all the hopes, comforts, and responsibilities of our salvation.
In that garden Your inspired Word is the seed
 that will bring forth good fruit according to its kind.[8]

---

1. Psalm 36:8-9
2. Hebrews 4:12
3. Jeremiah 17:9
4. John 15:3
5. Psalm 119:104-5
6. Psalm 19:7
7. Acts 4:13
8. Psalm 1:1-3

May Your Spirit enlighten our minds
    so we understand and obey Your Word.
May His light shine through us to needy people throughout the world
    so that they might recognize and submit to Your divine power.
No matter how great or how humble our labors,
    help us do them well as a blessing to You and others.
These things we ask, Father, in the name of Christ Your Son.

To You be all glory in the church
    and in Christ Jesus
        to all generations forever and ever.[1] Amen.

---

1. Ephesians 3:21

APPENDIX:

PRAYERS ON HOLY SEASONS

A CHRISTMAS PRAYER: PROCLAIMING CHRIST'S HUMBLE BIRTH

PHILIPPIANS 2:1-11

Therefore if there is any encouragement in Christ, if there is any consolation of love, if there is any fellowship of the Spirit, if any affection and compassion, make my joy complete by being of the same mind, maintaining the same love, united in spirit, intent on one purpose. Do nothing from selfishness or empty conceit, but with humility of mind regard one another as more important than yourselves; do not merely look out for your own personal interests, but also for the interests of others. Have this attitude in yourselves which was also in Christ Jesus, who, although He existed in the form of God, did not regard equality with God a thing to be grasped, but emptied Himself, taking the form of a bond-servant, and being made in the likeness of men. Being found in appearance as a man, He humbled Himself by becoming obedient to the point of death, even death on a cross. For this reason also, God highly exalted Him, and bestowed on Him the name which is above every name, so that at the name of Jesus every knee will bow, of those who are in heaven and on earth and under the earth, and that every tongue will confess that Jesus Christ is Lord, to the glory of God the Father.

OUR GREAT AND GRACIOUS GOD,

 no language on earth has words sufficient to give voice to our praise
  when we contemplate all that Christ has done for us.

How could we ever thank You enough
 for sending Your own dear Son from heaven to earth
 in the form of a lowly,
 common-born human baby to be our Redeemer and Substitute?
The fullness of His condescension and sacrifice,
 His humble obedience to the point of death—
 even death on a cross—
 is beyond our mind's grasp.
It makes us eager for the time
 when every knee will bow and every tongue will confess
  that Jesus Christ is Lord to Your glory, Father.

Heaven awaits a more suitable tribute
 than we are now capable of offering,
 and it will be our joy to fill all eternity with unbounded praise.

Our hearts are humbled and our minds taken captive
 by the reality that Christ left the glory of heaven
  to enter the world of humanity in so humble a fashion.
He was born like us, so that we might become like Him.
He made Himself a servant to show us how to lead.
He gave His life that we might live.
He suffered so that we can share in His glory.

We praise You for the ineffable wisdom of Christ's incarnation.
His person deity and humanity
 are united in an indivisible unity.
Thus He could die on our behalf as one of us, yet remain sinless.[1]
Now He intercedes for us as both God and man—
 the perfect mediator.[2]

---

1. Hebrews 2:14
2. 1 Timothy 2:5

He is Immanuel—God *with* us.[1]
He is the living proof that God is *for* us,
    and if our God is for us,
    we know that no one can prevail against us.[2]

Make these truths more precious in our sight
    than any of the empty pleasures of this world.
This world could never give any gift equal to the gift of Christ.

We confess, dear Father, that of all earthly creatures
    we are the least worthy to have Christ to become one of us
        and sacrifice His life for our redemption.
The enormity of our sin is a scandal.
The sheer number of our transgressions is staggering.
The many deliberate ways we have rebelled are shameful.
Our culpability is beyond question.
The weight of guilt that we have accumulated is frightful.
And yet Christ took the full burden of all our sin and disgrace
    and stood in our place to receive the due judgment.
Thanks be unto God for His unspeakable gift to us.[3]

In response we can only offer our highest words of praise—
    knowing how utterly feeble our best worship is,
    compared to the matchless worth of Christ.
Give us more suitable expressions of gratitude.
Fill us with hope and assurance.
Steady our erratic and error-prone walk.
Conform us to Christ's likeness and help us to walk in His steps.
And may our lives thus honor Him better
    than our tongues are able.
We ask these things in His blessed name. Amen.

---

1. Matthew 1:18-23
2. Romans 8:31
3. 2 Corinthians 9:15

AN EASTER PRAYER: SHARING IN CHRIST'S RESURRECTION LIFE

JOHN 20:1-18

Now on the first day of the week Mary Magdalene came early to the tomb, while it was still dark, and saw the stone already taken away from the tomb. So she ran and came to Simon Peter and to the other disciple whom Jesus loved, and said to them, "They have taken away the Lord out of the tomb, and we do not know where they have laid Him."

So Peter and the other disciple went forth, and they were going to the tomb. The two were running together; and the other disciple ran ahead faster than Peter and came to the tomb first; and stooping and looking in, he saw the linen wrappings lying there; but he did not go in. And so Simon Peter also came, following him, and entered the tomb; and he saw the linen wrappings lying there, and the face-cloth which had been on His head, not lying with the linen wrappings, but rolled up in a place by itself.

So the other disciple who had first come to the tomb then also entered, and he saw and believed. For as yet they did not understand the Scripture, that He must rise again from the dead. So the disciples went away again to their own homes. But Mary was standing outside the tomb weeping; and so, as she wept, she stooped and looked into the tomb; and she saw two angels in white sitting, one at the head and one at the feet, where the body of Jesus had been lying. And they said to her, "Woman, why are you weeping?"

She said to them, "Because they have taken away my Lord, and I do *not know where they have laid Him." When she had said this, she turned around and saw Jesus standing there, and did not know that it was Jesus.*

Jesus said to her, "Woman, why are you weeping? Whom are you seeking?"

Supposing Him to be the gardener, she said to Him, "Sir, if you have carried Him away, tell me where you have laid Him, and I will take Him away."

Jesus said to her, "Mary!"

She turned and said to Him in Hebrew, "Rabboni!" (which means, Teacher).

Jesus said to her, "Stop clinging to Me, for I have not yet ascended to the Father; but go to My brethren and say to them, 'I ascend to My Father and your Father, and My God and your God.'"

Mary Magdalene came, announcing to the disciples, "I have seen the Lord," and that He had said these things to her.

PRECIOUS FATHER, we marvel
    that You sent Your Son to redeem this fallen world.
We are filled with wonder at the thought
    that He took on human flesh
        and willingly experienced crucifixion, death, and burial.
We marvel even more that He rose from the dead.
The empty grave calls forth our adoring honor!
It is an emblem of assurance for us
    and the most vivid earthly symbol of heaven's hope.

We know beyond question that Christ rose bodily
    because all four Gospels attest to that fact.
Moreover, the apostles and hundreds of other eyewitnesses
    all faithfully proclaimed the truth of the resurrection.[1]

---

1. 1 Corinthians 15:3-8

Never was their testimony seriously challenged
    by contradictory witnesses,
      nor has their collective witness ever been refuted.
Rather, history vindicates it. The church affirms it.
The powerful influence of the gospel proves it conclusively.
Our hearts' experience knows it well,
    for just as Christ was raised physically from the dead
      by Your glory,
    we too were spiritually resurrected to walk in newness of life.[1]
The life we now live in the flesh
    we live by faith in the Son of God,
      who loved us and gave Himself for us.[2]

We thank You that our old self was crucified[3]
    so that we might live again.
May we earnestly seek to live always
    in the power of Christ's resurrection.[4]
May we devote all our energies
    to knowing Him who said,
      "I am the resurrection and the life;
      he who believes in Me will live even if he dies,
      and everyone who lives and believes in Me
        will never die."[5]

Christ's resurrection is the precious truth
    that vindicates His atoning work.
It is the seal of Your approval on the great sacrifice He offered—
    laying down His life for our sakes.
He was raised for our justification;[6]

1. Romans 6:4
2. Galatians 2:20
3. Romans 6:5
4. Philippians 3:10
5. John 11:25
6. Romans 4:25

brought up from the dead as proof our sins were fully forgiven.
Thus because of the resurrection we know with settled assurance
that all our transgressions have been removed from us
as far as the east is from the west.[1]

We thank You for that forgiveness, Father.
May we celebrate
not only by worshiping You now on our knees,
but also by never wandering from Your perfect will.

May we be both holy and full of joy
as we think about what it means to have life that is eternal
through union with the risen and ever-living Christ!
Grant us grace to persevere to the end.
May the truth and the power of the resurrection
permeate our thoughts,
control every aspect of our living,
and extend from us to those who will see
the glorious transformation of resurrection power.
We thank You for all You have done for Your people.
In the holy name of Christ we pray. Amen.

1. Psalm 103:12

OTHER GOOD HARVEST HOUSE READING WITH JOHN MACARTHUR

THE MAJESTY OF PRAYER
John MacArthur

Through prayer we can pour out our heart to God—our joys, concerns, hopes, and fears. We are invited to come before Him in intimate communion and to draw upon His infinite power, wisdom, and strength as the Lord of all creation.

Tune your heart to the prayers in these pages, and experience God's amazing grace in your life—a grace that satisfies and abounds to overflowing.

RIGHT THINKING IN A WORLD GONE WRONG
John MacArthur and the Leadership Team at Grace Community Church

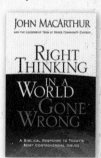

One of the greatest challenges facing Christians today is the powerful influence of secular thinking. From all directions we're fed a constant barrage of persuasive—yet unbiblical—worldviews.

The leadership team at Grace Community Church, along with their pastor, John MacArthur, provides much-needed discernment and clarity in the midst of confusion. Using the Bible as a foundation, you'll learn how to develop a Christian perspective on key issues, including political activism, environmentalism, homosexual marriage, abortion, euthanasia and suicide, immigration, disasters and epidemics, God and the problem of evil, and more.

BEING A DAD WHO LEADS
John MacArthur

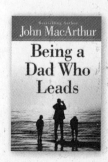

The rewards of being a dad who leads well are great. So what are the keys to effective leadership in the home? John pastor-teacher John MacArthur as he looks to Scripture for wisdom about…

- the starting point of a man's leadership—loving his wife
- keys to raising children who desire to follow God
- how to lovingly discipline children and nurture obedience
- traps to avoid in the course of parenting
- the power of a dad's example to influence future generations